MAN-MADE
DISASTERS

Building
Collapses

Titles in the Man-Made Disasters series include:

Airplane Crashes

Building Collapses

Nuclear Accidents

Oil and Chemical Spills

Shipwrecks

Tragedies of Space Exploration

MAN-MADE DISASTERS

Building Collapses

Mark Mayell

LUCENT
BOOKS®

THOMSON

™

GALE

San Diego • Detroit • New York • San Francisco • Cleveland • New Haven, Conn. • Waterville, Maine • London • Munich

© 2005 by Lucent Books. Lucent Books is an imprint of The Gale Group, Inc.,
a division of Thomson Learning, Inc.

Lucent Books® and Thomson Learning™ are trademarks used herein under license.

For more information, contact
Lucent Books
27500 Drake Rd.
Farmington Hills, MI 48331-3535
Or you can visit our Internet site at http://www.gale.com

LIBRARY OF CONGRESS CATALOGING-IN-PUBLICATION DATA

Mayell, Mark.
  Building collapses / by Mark Mayell.
     p. cm. — (Man-made disasters)
  Includes bibliographical references and index.
  ISBN 1-59018-055-0 (hardcover : alk. paper)
  1. Building failures—Juvenile literature. I. Title. II. Series.
TH441.M383 2004
690--dc22

                                                                2004010843

Printed in the United States of America

Contents

Foreword

In the late 1990s a University of Florida study came to a surprising conclusion. Researchers determined that the local residents they surveyed were more afraid of nuclear accidents, chemical spills, and other man-made disasters than they were of natural disasters such as hurricanes and floods. This finding seemed especially odd given that natural disasters are often much more devastating than man-made disasters, at least in terms of human lives. The collapse of the two World Trade Center towers on September 11, 2001, was among the worst human-caused disasters in recent memory, yet even its horrific death toll of roughly three thousand pales in comparison to, for example, the 1976 earthquake in China that killed an estimated seven hundred thousand people.

How then does one explain people's overarching fear of man-made disasters? One factor mentioned by the Florida researchers related to the widespread perception that natural hazards are "acts of God" that no one can control. Earthquakes, forest fires, and the like are thus accepted as inevitable. Man-made disasters are viewed differently, as unpredictable yet maddeningly preventable. Even worse, because these new technologies are so incredibly complex—a 747 airliner has 6 million parts, the one-hundred-foot-long control room of a nuclear power plant has thousands of gauges and controls—the root cause of the disaster can often be shockingly trivial. One notorious 1972 airliner crash occurred when a tiny lightbulb, the indicator for whether the nose landing gear was down, burned out. While in flight, the captain, copilot, and engineer decided to replace the bulb. With the crew distracted, someone in the cockpit accidentally disengaged the autopilot and the plane flew into the ground, killing 98 of 176 on board.

Man-made disasters are also distressing because they are so furtive in their deadliness. The hazardous radiation emitted by the nuclear accident at Tokaimura, Japan, in 1999 could neither be seen nor smelled, and the lethal gas that leaked from a Union Carbide pesticide factory in India in 1984 settled silently over the city of Bhopal, killing thousands in their homes.

Another factor may be the widespread perception that man-made disasters are worse than ever. This is probably true although faulty designs and shoddy workmanship have been causing building collapses, dam failures, and ship sinkings for thousands of years. Beginning with the twentieth century, new industrial technology, such as nuclear power and oil refining, can affect huge areas over many years when something goes wrong. The radiation from the disaster at the Chernobyl nuclear power plant in 1986 spread worldwide and has closed local areas to human habitation to this day. Finally, man-made disasters have begun to compound each other: In January 1997, a massive oil spill caused by the shipwreck of a Russian tanker in the Sea of Japan threatened to clog crucial cooling systems in nearby nuclear power plants.

Fortunately, humanity can learn vital lessons from man-made disasters. Practical insights mean that ocean liners no longer ply the seas, as the *Titanic* did, with too few lifeboats and no ability to see in the dark. Nuclear power plants are not being built with the type of tin-can containment building that Chernobyl had. The latest generation of oil tankers has double hulls, which should vastly reduce oil spills. On the more philosophical level, man-made disasters offer valuable insights into issues relating to progress and technology, risk and safety, and government and corporate responsibility.

The Man-Made Disasters series presents a clear and up-to-date overview of such dramatic events as airplane crashes, nuclear accidents, oil and chemical spills, tragedies of space exploration, shipwrecks, and building collapses. Each book in the series serves as both a wide-ranging introduction and a guide to further study. Fully documented primary and secondary source quotes enliven the narrative. Sidebars highlight important events, personalities, and technologies. Annotated bibliographies provide readers with ideas for further research. Finally, the many facts and unforgettable stories relate the hubris—pride bordering on arrogance—as well as the resiliency of daring pioneers, bold innovators, brave rescuers, and lucky survivors.

Towers of Terror

I n the early morning hours of November 11, 1999, tenants in a six-story apartment building in Foggia, Italy, were awakened by loud cracking sounds. Some of the residents quickly realized that their worst fears—fears they had been voicing to local officials for the previous two years—were coming true. Their building was about to collapse. Rushing from their apartments, many residents knocked on neighbors' doors, trying to awaken and warn others. Fifteen people escaped down the stairs and out of the building just minutes before it collapsed with a sickening crash of concrete and metal. All of the remaining sixty-seven residents were killed. A subsequent medical study determined that approximately half the victims sustained fatal injuries and half died from asphyxia, smothered as they were trapped, broken and bleeding, in the rubble heap.

The Foggia tragedy occurred less than a year after a collapse in another Italian apartment building, in Rome, had killed twenty-seven. Italian officials admitted that more than 3 million houses in the country were at risk for similar such collapses, because of either age or shoddy construction that was widespread during a recent building boom. Foggia seemed especially tragic because tenants' complaints about the building's safety had gone unheeded. Engineers had even examined the building days before the collapse, and assured the residents that the structure was safe.

A Common Tragedy Worldwide

The investigators who researched the Foggia and Rome disasters discovered design, construction, and siting flaws in the buildings, all of which contributed to the unexpected collapses. In the absence of earthquake or other natural disaster, such

major catastrophes with scores of deaths are relatively rare. Yet thousands of buildings collapse worldwide every year, with many causing fatalities or serious injuries. Within just a few months during 2002, for example, a thirty-year-old apartment building suddenly collapsed in St. Petersburg, Russia, killing four (investigators discovered that the builders had omitted a number of concrete blocks from the foundation); a multistory building in downtown Beirut, Lebanon, collapsed into a pile of rubble, killing four (possibly from faulty restoration work being done); and a four-story building collapsed in Damietta, Egypt, killing twenty-two (the building's owner had made unlicensed modifications). The sprawling city of Bombay, India, experiences close to one house or building collapse per day.

Many of the worst such collapses occur in developing nations but the United States is hardly immune. A 2003 study identified a total of 225 building failures (unrelated to natural

▲ Scores of Italian rescue workers search for survivors of the Foggia apartment building collapse.

▲ Residents evacuated this nine-story apartment building in St. Petersburg, Russia, shortly before it collapsed.

disasters) in the United States from 1989 to 2000. "Far from declining," noted the organizers of an international meeting on defective building, "both the frequency and severity of building failures are on the increase. Buildings, building systems, and facilities are more sophisticated, new materials and techniques are constantly introduced, and construction times are cut ever so short."[1] As the attacks on the Alfred P. Murrah Federal Building in Oklahoma City in April 1995, the World Trade Center towers in September 2001, and the United Nations compound in Baghdad in August 2003 demonstrated, terrorism is an increasing concern for its potential to collapse buildings worldwide.

Of course, the vast majority of building collapses happen not from construction errors, faulty renovation, or terrorist attack but as the result of earthquakes, hurricanes, tornadoes, and floods. One estimate is that approximately thirty thousand buildings in the United States alone suffer collapse or significant structural damage from such natural disasters each year, at a cost to the nation of $10 billion and 150 lives. A single tornado that struck Oklahoma City in May 1999 destroyed almost three thousand homes and apartments and killed forty-nine people. Worldwide, the death toll from earthquakes is shocking—approximately 2 million people during the twentieth century alone. Collapsing buildings caused the vast majority of these deaths.

Learning from Collapses

While earthquakes and hurricanes cannot be prevented, many buildings manage to survive them. Clearly, the effects of natural disasters on buildings can be reduced at least partially by architectural, engineering, and construction decisions. Addressing factors such as defective building materials, poorly executed work, and substandard building codes is an ongoing concern within the building industry as well as the larger society. Much can be learned about building safety and survival during catastrophes by looking at how buildings are constructed, what keeps them standing, and why they sometimes collapse.

CHAPTER ONE

The Sound and the Fury

The sudden collapse of a building is a shocking and frightening occurrence, a nightmare of falling debris and tumbling bodies. Buildings collapse for various reasons and in different ways. The scale of the disaster can range from the collapse of a single small building to the simultaneous collapse of multiple structures over an extended area, as from an earthquake. The actual experience of those inside a collapsing building, however, may be most affected by whether the building is a skyscraper like the two World Trade Center (WTC) towers, a smaller multistory office building, or a one- or two-story home.

An Unthinkable Impact

The two commercial-jet terrorist attacks on the WTC skyscrapers on September 11, 2001, resulted in by far the single worst collapse of buildings in history. Never before had such immense buildings, crowded with thousands of people, fallen so quickly and disastrously. But never before had skyscrapers been hit with such blows. The terrorists piloting the hijacked planes, both Boeing 767s en route from Boston to Los Angeles, plunged them into the buildings at approximately 470 and 590 miles per hour. Because each plane was carrying an estimated ten thousand gallons of jet fuel at impact, the explosions were massive, packing a punch equal to about half a million pounds of TNT.

The North Tower, WTC-1, was hit first, at 8:46 on a Tuesday morning. It was early enough that the building was perhaps only half full, with an estimated five to seven thousand workers and visitors. American Airlines Flight 11, carrying ninety-two people, crashed into the tower at a slight angle, destroying much of floors ninety-three through ninety-eight. Jet fuel from the impact led to uncontrollable fires in the damaged floors, with temperatures exceeding two thousand degrees Fahrenheit. The building's three staircases were rendered impassable to lower floors and all of the elevators were inoperable.

United Airlines Flight 175, carrying sixty-five people, struck the South Tower, WTC-2, at 9:03 A.M. The crucial seventeen-minute interval between impacts ultimately led to much less loss of life among those in this tower. More than a thousand people were able to evacuate from the upper floors of WTC-2, many taking advantage of an efficient elevator system that was among the best in the world. The airliner hit

◀ Smoke rises following the collapse of the two WTC towers. Many of the buildings surrounding the site also collapsed.

WTC-2 at a sharp angle, destroying much of floors seventy-eight through eighty-four.

Brian Clark, a financial executive who was working on the eighty-fourth floor of WTC-2, reported that the impact collapsed his office's ceiling, buckled floor tiles, and tore apart walls. "For seven to ten seconds there was this enormous sway in the building," he said. "It was one way, and I just felt in my heart, *Oh my gosh, we are going over.* That's what it felt like . . . I thought it was over—horrible feeling—but then the building righted itself."[2] Clark was one of only four survivors in either tower from above the floors struck by the aircraft. They were able to make a harrowing hour-long descent through smoke, fire, noise, confusion, and destruction only because, unlike in WTC-1, one stairwell remained passable through the destroyed floors.

Apocalypse Now

The towers were easily strong and flexible enough to snap back from the immediate impacts—the buildings were too massive to fall anywhere but straight down—but the crisis was just beginning for those occupants still alive. The so-called smokestack effect caused smoke to rise through elevator shafts and stairwells. The overhead-sprinkler fire systems were wiped out on the crash floors, and probably higher. The intense fires drove many of those people still alive on upper floors to the tops of the two buildings. Any hope for rescue by helicopter was quashed by the rising columns of intense heat and thick smoke. Some people chose to jump to a certain death. Meanwhile hundreds of firefighters, police officers, and emergency personnel poured into the two buildings and started to climb the stairs in a heroic rescue attempt.

With horrifying suddenness, one minute before 10:00 A.M., WTC-2 thundered to the ground. Thousands had escaped, but 599 people who were in the tower at the time of the airliner impact died. Only four of these deaths were to people who worked below the crash floors.

After the collapse of WTC-2, the evacuation of WTC-1 took on a heart-thumping urgency for occupants and emergency personnel. Many of those trapped on upper floors held little hope for rescue. "I've got five people here. We can't get out,"[3] related a man in a call from a suite on the ninetieth floor of WTC-1 to the Port Authority of New York and New Jersey, the

A CLASSIC PANCAKE COLLAPSE

Buildings tend to collapse by tumbling sideways, tenting inward, or pancaking downward. The WTC towers fell in a classic progressive pancake, with the weight of upper floors collapsing those below them. Each building fell in a mere ten seconds. Debris from upper floors hit the ground at a speed of 125 miles per hour, only marginally slower than a free fall. The collapse impacts were great enough to register with the force of small earthquakes on seismic monitors twenty miles north of Manhattan.

▲ WTC-1 disintegrates into a cloud of dust and debris in a matter of seconds.

agency that manages the World Trade Center. Some people panicked, some made poignant goodbye calls to loved ones.

Hundreds of others in offices below the crash floors were still trying to escape. Genelle Guzman-McMillan, a Trinidad-born Port Authority clerk, had tarried with a group of fifteen others at their sixty-fourth-floor offices in WTC-1, unsure whether to evacuate. Finally, shortly after 10:00 A.M., they headed down stairwell B, passing groups of firefighters on the way up. (After WTC-2 collapsed, fire department commanders on the ground sent out a recall, but some firefighters never got the message.) The Port Authority workers were at the thirteenth floor when they heard a huge noise, what one survivor later described as "a dozen safes being tossed down the stairs"[4] and a firefighter likened to "being on a locomotive track with a train coming at you."[5] WTC-1 had managed to stand twenty-nine minutes longer than its twin, but it was now collapsing. Guzman-McMillan was "jostled like a pinball and struck by debris from everywhere," noted *Time* writer John Cloud in a vivid, you-are-there report:

> As the great noise begins to subside, she is lying on her right side, and her right leg is pinned hard. Her head is now caught between something—the floor maybe?—and some concrete. Finally, it's all quiet, and it's dark, but somehow she is here. She is alive. Soon she says the first of many prayers, asking God to continue to shepherd her to safety. Not far away, a man is calling, "Help! Help!" His voice falters and disappears. She won't hear him again.[6]

Of the 1,360 people who were at or above the ninety-second floor in WTC-1 when the building was struck by the airliner, none survived. Another 72 among the 4,000 or so in lower floors were also killed. The double catastrophe also claimed the lives of 403 firefighters, policemen, and emergency personnel. An additional 10 people on the ground

▼ The collapse of the two WTC towers left massive rubble piles at ground zero.

were killed by falling debris, while the remainder of the 2,752 total WTC fatalities could not be attributed to a specific building.

Under the Debris

What came to be known as ground zero was a nightmarish scene of twisted steel, pulverized concrete, and human remains. Surgeon Jennifer Svahn, on the rubble heap to help victims, said there were none—"There's a morgue down there, and body parts. It's a crematorium."[7] Actually there were eighteen survivors among the more than two thousand people who were still alive in the buildings when they collapsed. Most of the fortunate survivors were in a group of fourteen firefighters and others who pulled through in a lower-floor stairwell of WTC-1.

The massive piles of rubble were five stories high (perhaps not as high as many might have expected, but the buildings were actually about 95 percent empty space) and each weighed one-half million tons. The disaster scene covered almost twenty acres. Researchers quickly realized that it would take weeks or even months to reach the bottom of the pile, which was unstable, on fire, and emitting toxic fumes. Within the first few hours of the rescue effort, emergency personnel began to suspect that there was little hope that more than a few people could have survived the collapse. "There's no concrete there," commented New York City firefighter Brenda Berkman. She continued:

> You'd expect that there would be enormous pieces of concrete. There are just tiny chunks. The rebar [round steel bars used to reinforce concrete] has been stripped clean. It's just pieces of twisted metal, packed down dust and paper, and rubbish, and that's it. There is no glass—not a piece of glass, and the World Trade Center Towers were 20 percent glass. Everything was just pulverized.[8]

Guzman-McMillan was the final ground zero survivor to be found, rescued twenty-six hours after the collapse of WTC-1. She was pinned so tightly under the rubble that she could barely move her head. Hard objects poked into her from all around, though she also felt something soft near her leg. It was the body of a dead fireman. After a painful day and night, she managed to bang a chunk of debris against concrete. According to Cloud, this attracted the attention of rescuers "drawn to her spot in the vast acres of destruction by a firefighter's uniform. Civilian clothes blend with the rubble, but reflective bands in the uniforms stand out. There is a uniform just below Genelle: the soft man. It takes 20 long minutes, and then she is saved."[9]

As the days after Guzman-McMillan's rescue ticked by, ground zero workers sadly accepted that only human remains were left to be found.

A Superstore Collapse in South Korea

The collapse of skyscrapers like the WTC towers is the ultimate hell-on-earth, with the many lethal threats creating an

▶ South Korea's Sampoong department store was full of shoppers when it suddenly collapsed in June 1995.

▲ Rescue workers at Sampoong lift a stretcher bearing a collapse survivor.

almost unsurvivable scene. The collapse of smaller, but still multistory, apartment or office buildings can be just as frightening and nearly as deadly. That was certainly the case in one of the worst accidental building collapses in modern history, suffered by South Korea's Sampoong Superstore, a large and swanky department store that opened in the capital city of Seoul in 1989.

The collapse was preceded by numerous warning signs that were ignored or downplayed by the building's owners. Cracks suddenly appeared in walls, water seeped though ceilings, and gas leaked into departments. On June 29, 1995, building owners brought in structural engineers for an appraisal. The engineers' findings were alarming: The building was unsafe and needed to be evacuated. The store's owners moved some merchandise around, and allowed some executives to leave the building, but they did not warn customers or close the store.

FINDING THE TRIANGLES OF LIFE

The conventional "duck and cover" advice about how to survive a building collapse has been challenged by a new approach developed by rescue expert Douglas Copp, founder of Albuquerque, New Mexico–based American Rescue Team International. His "triangle of life" method is to recognize and move into spaces that can be expected to become voids when ceilings fall upon sturdy objects or furniture. In an ambassador's office where there was a large steel safe, Copp once said, "If an earthquake should occur and completely destroy this building, killing every single person inside, I will survive because I will be in the space next to this safe."

A revealing test conducted in Istanbul, Turkey, placed ten dummies in duck-and-cover positions inside a building, along with ten in triangles of life. The building was then collapsed. Rescuers who crawled into the wreckage described the duck-and-cover dummies as "ducked and splattered" while the triangle of life ones were untouched. Rescuers say that adopting the new method may increase building collapse survival from the current rate of 2 percent to as high as 95 percent.

Shortly before 6:00 P.M. that evening, the nine-story (five upper and four basement floors) luxury complex was full of shoppers when it caved in with devastating force. A cabdriver parked in front said, "It just folded as if it was being destroyed by a demolition crew, the way you see on television."[10] The dinnertime collapse killed 501 of the building's occupants, many of whom were congregated in a food area in the basement. More than 900 others were injured, many seriously.

When a representative of the country's ruling political party visited the collapse scene to speak to those waiting for news of victims, angry citizens beat him up. Their suspicions about the role of political corruption in the collapse proved to be correct. Subsequent investigations into the Sampoong disaster identified a number of culprits, including two dozen local officials charged with taking bribes. The owner of the department store and his son, the store's president, were found guilty of criminal negligence and sentenced to seven-year jail terms.

Death from Above

The almost complete collapse of large buildings such as the Foggia apartment building and the Seoul department store are relatively rare. It is much more common for parts of a building to fail, as when a section of a supermarket roof caves in after a snowstorm, or a balcony overloaded with people collapses. In fact one of the most famous building failures in history, an event that inspired widespread reforms, was a partial collapse. It occurred on May 16, 1968, in Canning Town, outside of London.

Ivy Hodge awakened early that morning in her apartment on the eighteenth floor of the new twenty-two-story Ronan Point tower. She went into her kitchen to make tea and put a match to the burner of her gas stove. Hodge survived the resulting gas leak explosion with second-degree burns but five

◀ A minor gas explosion led to the deadly Ronan Point corner collapse.

other residents in the tower were not so lucky. That is because the building's design and its prefab construction permitted a relatively small amount of force—the blast had not even damaged Hodge's eardrums—to blow out two walls of her corner living room. As the wall panels fell 180 feet to the ground, the living room on the nineteenth floor collapsed, and then the one above it and so on up to the top of the building. The weight of these walls and floors as they fell caused a progressive collapse of the entire corner of the tower.

"The whole place shook," James Chambers, who was in his bedroom with his wife in a seventh-floor apartment, says in Phillip Wearne's *Collapse*. He adds:

> Suddenly our bedroom wall fell away with a terrible ripping sound. We found ourselves staring out over London, our heads just two feet away from the eighty-foot drop. Showers of debris and furniture were plunging past us. We heard screams. I think it must have been someone falling with the debris.[11]

The screams the Chambers heard may have come from the couple who were killed when the bedroom floor in their top-floor apartment gave way. The death toll would have been much higher had the collapse occurred later in the day, when more of the residents might have been in their living rooms, which below the eighteenth story were the main part of the apartments destroyed.

"There Was No Warning"

No such reprieve was available to the victims of a lethal partial collapse that occurred at a three-story dwelling in Chicago on June 29, 2003. Late-night partygoers had crowded onto three porches that extended off the back of the apartment house, located in an affluent neighborhood. The third-story porch was crammed with more than forty young people, many of them former classmates from an area high school. This crowd was perhaps twice as large, however, as the wooden structure was designed to hold. With a crack of timbers, the porch collapsed. Seven men and six women, mostly on porches directly below, were killed as people and lumber crashed to the ground. Dozens more were injured, some seriously.

"All of a sudden, I saw all these heads going down," recalled a witness who was in the kitchen next to the collapsing

◄ The collapse of an overloaded third-story porch killed thirteen people in Chicago in June 2003.

porch. "The floor just dropped out from underneath them. They all went down in unison."[12]

"There was no warning," said one of the collapse survivors, University of Chicago law student Simon Rasin. "I fell through both the second and the first floor decks into the basement area in just a pile of bodies."[13]

Accident investigators identified severe overloading as the main cause of the Chicago porch collapse. Partial building collapses and balcony failures may also be due to weathering of exterior building components. For example, a balcony on a Thomas Jefferson–designed University of Virginia building that collapsed during the school's 1997 graduation ceremony, killing one and injuring two dozen others, failed due to corrosion in one of the original wrought iron support rods.

When the Earth Quakes

The Ronan Point and Chicago porch collapses were typical in that more people experience building collapses at home than anywhere else. The most common reason for these collapses, however, is not shoddy construction or overcrowding but rather the prevalence and frequency of earthquakes around the world. An earthquake can within a few seconds collapse buildings over a widespread area. Earthquakes have plagued humanity since ancient times, and the vast majority of earthquake-related deaths are due to building collapses. Because cities have become larger and populations more concentrated, earthquake-related building collapses—predominantly houses—presently kill more people than any other type of disaster. Earthquake-caused multiple-building collapses now rank among the deadliest threats in human history—at least 250,000 and possibly as many as 700,000 people perished from the earthquake that struck Tangshan (Tianjin), China, in July 1976.

Earthquakes can collapse buildings in a number of ways. When the ground suddenly shifts sideways, a building's foundation may crumble. Walls that are not firmly anchored into the foundation may splay. Buildings on or near hills can be hit by landslides triggered by the quakes. Seismic waves are amplified as they pass through certain soils, shaking buildings apart and collapsing adjacent buildings into each other.

Another danger is that when an earthquake strikes loose or sandy soil, the ground may temporarily act much like a liquid. Lacking firm support, a building's foundations or support columns may be undermined, allowing the building to topple sideways. The violent earthquake that devastated much of Mexico City on September 19, 1985, crumbled some eight hundred buildings at least in part because of the city's location on a former lake bed. Mexico City's birth can be traced to the mid–fourteenth century, when the Aztecs sited their capital city of Tenochtitlan, for defensive purposes, on an island. The lake was gradually drained as Mexico City later developed into one of the most densely populated urban areas in the world. The loose sedimentary soil underlying the city's many tall buildings, however, is notoriously unstable during an earthquake. In 1985, hospitals, schools, and apartment buildings collapsed in Mexico City even though the earthquake's epicenter was more than two hundred miles to the west.

Disaster in Japan

Whether a building can survive an earthquake depends not only on the type of underlying earth but on various other factors, particularly how it was designed and constructed. Many of the estimated ten thousand earthquake-related deaths in Mexico City occurred in seven- to fifteen-story concrete buildings that had been constructed in the previous forty years without sufficient concern for seismic strength. Buildings swayed until supports cracked, or adjacent buildings knocked into each other.

Earthquakes that devastate rural areas may claim most of their victims in shorter, unreinforced masonry buildings. Such structures are made of brick, stone, adobe, concrete block, or hollow clay tiles without the use of steel reinforcement bars for additional structural support. Traditionally built homes using sun-dried mud bricks for walls, supporting heavy roofs, become death traps during an earthquake. Cheaply built, modern unreinforced masonry buildings with large glass windows for ground-floor stores are also especially vulnerable to an earthquake's lateral shaking, with collapses being particularly lethal to ground-floor occupants. In some earthquake-prone areas, older unreinforced masonry buildings that incorporate traditional design features, such as occasional wooden spacers between the masonry layers, have proven to be strong and flexible enough to survive most earthquakes.

During one of the worst earthquakes in recent history, in Kobe, Japan, in January 1995, a person was much safer in the top floor of a modern skyscraper than in the kitchen of a single-family home. Of the sixty-four hundred people killed in the Kobe earthquake, an estimated 90 percent died from the direct result of building collapse. (The remainder were mainly from fire.) Twenty thousand Japanese were crushed or trapped in collapsed buildings. More than one hundred thousand homes and apartments were destroyed, or subsequently had to be demolished.

Most of the Kobe-area buildings that collapsed were one- and two-story buildings, many of them constructed from wood rather than masonry during the country's postwar building boom of the 1950s. The high cost of lumber in Japan, however, meant that many of these houses used fewer roof beams and wall supports than do wooden homes in, for example, California. The lack of structural support contributed to a high collapse rate. Moreover, the traditional tile roofs on Japanese homes are relatively heavy. This allows the roofs to resist high winds from the frequent typhoons, but the extra weight also makes tile roofs more prone to come crashing down during an earthquake.

The extent of the death and destruction due to the Kobe earthquake surprised many Japanese. "In fact," noted *National Geographic* writer T.R. Reid, "some officials had boasted that Japanese architecture was earthquake proof—a claim that turned to dust in the rubble of Kobe."[14] Thousands of homes turned out to be very vulnerable to collapse during the

▼ Survivors of the Kobe earthquake salvage belongings across the street from a burning, partially collapsed building.

A BOSTON FIREFIGHTER'S CLOSE CALL

In District Fire Chief Robert Winston's vivid first-person account, he describes the chaotic scene he witnessed at a three-story, wood-frame apartment building in Boston in August 1998. Observing "heavy fire and smoke conditions, a strong odor of natural gas, a crowd of dazed people, street construction, blast debris in the street, and Ladder 29's aerial raised to a third-floor window," with one firefighter at the tip of the aerial ladder and another inside the partially destroyed building, he ordered an immediate evacuation. "I watched as the two firefighters from Ladder 29 descended their aerial ladder and reached the ground to safety. It was then and without warning that the entire three-decker collapsed with a roar in a cloud of dust and smoke! From the time I radioed the evacuation order and watched the two firefighters get off the aerial ladder, it was about one minute or so. We all stood there for a moment kind of transfixed at what just occurred."

1995 earthquake, although the modern skyscrapers and most (though not all) of the multistory office buildings that had sprouted up in the Kobe area within recent years fared much better. Experts believe that a number of building reforms put in place for high-rise buildings after the catastrophic Tokyo earthquake of 1923, which killed a staggering 143,000 people, made a difference. These reforms included a seismic design requirement that has served as a model for other earthquake-prone areas.

Beyond the Shock

Whether a building collapse is caused by human error or natural disaster, being inside a building as it unexpectedly collapses is a horrifying experience, one that few people have experienced and lived to tell about. For survivors, the initial sense of shock and fear often soon turns to bewilderment and dismay—How could this have happened? Identifying the underlying causes of any building collapse requires first and foremost a basic understanding of how a building supports itself against the physical forces constantly acting upon it.

CHAPTER TWO

Why Buildings Collapse

Most people think of buildings as massive, inanimate objects, like giant rocks. In fact buildings are more aptly compared to living things, complex entities that move (the top floors of a skyscraper may sway many feet with the wind) and "breathe" (buildings exchange gases with the environment). Like living things, buildings are also part of, and intimately affected by, their natural environment. This includes the many physical forces—what engineers refer to as "loads"—that can be destructive either suddenly or over time.

Architects, engineers, and builders are aware of these varied forces and take them into consideration during every stage of a building's life. Loads play a role in how a building is designed, where it is located, what materials and methods are used in its construction, and how it is maintained and used. The concern with safely handling potential physical loads must be balanced, however, by other factors. These include a host of practical considerations, ranging from a building's cost to its aesthetics—how it looks and feels to occupants and the community. Building design and construction is thus both an art and a science, requiring compromise and cooperation to reach a successful final structure. As with any human endeavor, seemingly minor faults in the process can on occasion contribute to a chain of events that seems inevitably to lead to a collapse.

Static, Dynamic, and Hidden Loads

Buildings must be sturdy enough to deal with three main types of loads, known as static, dynamic, and hidden. The first of these, static loads, are more or less constant. Engineers find it useful to further distinguish such constant loads as "dead" or "live." Dead load is the weight of the building itself, including walls, floors, and roof. A heavier building is stronger in the wind, but the weight of upper floors also puts added strain on lower floors. The live load is the sum total of what is put into a building—furniture, people, equipment, and so forth. Live load may change, but usually slowly and within relatively narrow margins. If an existing building is renovated for a new purpose, however, the live load may increase dramatically, raising the risk of a collapse. For example, an office building might require major structural changes to be used as a warehouse.

Dynamic loads act upon buildings more suddenly. For example, high winds or an earthquake can cause a building to suddenly twist or shift on its foundation. An explosion in or next to a building, or a vehicle or aircraft crashing into a building, is a dramatic dynamic load. A number of history's major building disasters were due to accidental lightning strikes causing explosions of stored gunpowder. The worst such incident was probably the April 3, 1856, explosion that obliterated a church and adjacent palace in Rhodes, Greece, killing four thousand people.

WHY THERE ARE NO ALL-BRICK SKYSCRAPERS

Dead load becomes more and more of a concern as buildings soar higher. If walls are weight bearing, for example, they have to be much stronger at street level than at upper floors in order to support all the weight that is pushing down from above. This can limit the height of buildings with weight-bearing stone or brick walls, by requiring overly thick street-level walls. Such is the case with Chicago's famous Monadnock Building, finished in 1893. At sixteen floors, it is the world's tallest brick, wall-bearing skyscraper. It manages this, however, only by having six-foot-thick walls at its base! First-floor windows and doors, as a result, are tunnel-like.

▲ Chicago's Monadnock Building is distinguished by massive street-level walls.

Hidden loads, such as the daily and seasonal stresses a building faces from changes in temperature, are active but less sudden. Steel, concrete, bricks, and other building materials expand from the heat of direct sunlight, and contract from cold. Building designs may have to consider the varying effects of temperature changes on adjacent materials, since cracks or scaling can lead to structural weakness. Acid rain can dissolve materials, especially limestone. Salt from the oceans can corrode metals and other components of seaside buildings. Humidity can promote harmful chemical changes in building materials. Fluctuations in the water table beneath a building, such as from human pumping of groundwater for irrigation or other use, may alter soil composition and weaken the building's stability.

Dealing with Extremes

▼ A devastating tornado that struck Gainesville, Georgia, in April 1936 collapsed the town's city hall building.

Static, dynamic, and hidden loads must be calculated and planned for during design, construction, and maintenance to make sure a building will be safe to occupy. However, predict-

ing how various loads will interact, even when using sophisticated computer technology and high-tech facilities such as wind tunnels, can be difficult. This is because building designs, sites, and materials are infinitely variable.

Moreover, natural forces can be complex and powerful. Consider wind, which is the most common source of damage and destruction to houses. A basic wind speed (expected on average at least once every fifty years) of 70 miles per hour exists throughout almost the entire United States, strong enough to cause minor structural damage to aging chimneys and roofs. Most of the coastal regions from the Gulf of Mexico to Maine are classified as 100-mile-per-hour or higher basic wind speed zones. Even more severe wind speeds occur during some hurricanes, like the 150-mile-per-hour Andrew that caused $25 billion worth of damage to Florida in August 1992. Designing and building structures that can resist hurricane-force winds promises to become increasingly important as more people and buildings congregate in coastal areas. Demographers predict that by the year 2025 three out of every four Americans will live in coastal counties.

The most extreme winds, of course, are found in tornadoes, and the United States happens to be the tornado capital of the world. About a thousand touch down annually, mostly in the central portion of the country. Scientists estimate top speeds of 250 to 300 miles per hour in the strongest tornadoes, which will completely blow away even strongly built homes. Tornadoes kill an average of one hundred Americans annually and destroy or collapse billions of dollars worth of buildings.

Design: Balancing Safety and Economy

How best to design and build for such extreme albeit occasional winds is only the first challenge. Wind effects on buildings can be magnified by factors such as a building's height, shape, weight, and openings; the surrounding landscape; and the size and shape of nearby buildings. Venturi effects, named after a nineteenth-century Italian physicist, occur when wind is forced to squeeze between two objects, whether mountains or buildings, greatly magnifying its speed. Slow but constant winds can cause fatigue of building components. Gusts that suddenly change direction can twist and rack a building. Slender buildings under the influence of moderate winds may begin to sway back and forth, achieving a resonance that can reach dangerous extremes.

Designers must also strike a balance between safety and cost. Thus, for example, an architect may determine that a building has a one-in-one-hundred chance of facing a 100-mile-per-hour wind during its lifetime, and should therefore be strong enough to withstand a 150-mile-per-hour wind. The building could be designed to resist a once-a-millennium 200-mile-per-hour wind, but at such great cost as to be impractical.

Given the complexities and conflicting demands, it is not surprising that architects and structural engineers sometimes err when they try to predict the types and the magnitudes of the loads that a building may face. The margin for error or "factors of safety" that structural engineers insert into their plans to protect against disasters have even been incorporated into building codes, which are typically locally mandated regulations for design and construction. Factors of safety ideally result in buildings that can resist much higher forces than they realistically expect to face. Nevertheless, problems arise. Small errors by the designer, for example, may be compounded by additional errors during the manufacturing of building components, site construction or renovation, inspection, and so forth. According to engineer Dov Kaminetzky, "Much of the problem usually is the human element of constructing the building."[15]

Waiting for Gravity

In numerous instances, design problems have been magnified by further faulty decisions. A notable example led to the Ronan Point partial collapse. That apartment tower was one of some six hundred similar buildings constructed in Great Britain to help relieve a housing shortage and to clear inner-city slums. The factory-based, system-built construction method, developed in the late 1940s, was economically efficient and structurally simple, making use of prefabricated, reinforced concrete wall and floor panels. Like a house of cards, the one-story-tall walls were stacked atop floors at the building site. The building had no frame as such, merely the weight-bearing walls. How walls are connected to floors takes on added importance in such buildings, since any force that caused a single wall to move or bend outward could displace the wall above and possibly lead to a progressive collapse.

BEHIND THE BUSINESS OF BUILDING DEMOLITION

Seeing a massive, unwanted building intentionally crashed to the ground is undeniably spectacular, as tens of thousands of tons of brick or concrete plunge earthward, the ground shakes, and a roaring cloud of dust billows outward. Behind the spectacle, however, is a great deal of experience and technical knowledge that demolition companies must possess in order to direct the collapse. How these intentional building collapses are accomplished, moreover, can offer useful insights into why buildings sometimes fall down on their own.

Demolition engineers need to carefully study a building's skeleton—where structural supports are placed and what they are made of—before placing any explosives. They look at blueprints and inspect the building to identify the structure's supporting elements. The building materials will determine what type of explosive to use: conventional dynamite to take out reinforced concrete columns, a more high-velocity explosive known as RDX for steel beams. Whatever the explosive, placement and timing are crucial. Most demolitions require numerous separately spaced charges set off in a precise sequence over a few seconds. Ground-floor supports are typically taken out first, with additional upper floor explosions following to promote breakage as the building falls. If there is a parking lot or other open space next to the building, the building is collapsed in that direction by first destroying the supports on one side of the building. Imploding a building—bringing it down on its own footprint—is somewhat trickier, requiring that supports in the center of a building be taken out first.

▲ Well-timed explosives demolish a St. Louis apartment building in 1972.

This is exactly what happened when one apartment had an accidental gas explosion, breaking the flimsy bolts that held wall to floor and thus undermining the support for upper stories. The government inquiry into the Ronan Point disaster made a number of practical recommendations, ranging from reinforcing wall-to-floor joints to replacing gas stoves with electric ones. Eventually, the building's collapsed corner was reconstructed and residents moved back in. Skeptics like Sam Webb, however, remained wary. A junior architect for the local housing authority, Webb noted that the prefab construction method was originally intended only for buildings up to six stories in height, not for twenty-two-story skyscrapers like Ronan Point. Webb and other safety advocates charged that officials were minimizing the ongoing dangers to Ronan Point residents, as well as to the residents of many similarly constructed buildings.

Much as Webb feared, in the early 1980s Ronan Point began showing premature signs of wear. Gaps formed between walls and floors. Cracks appeared in the central staircase and elevator shaft. "For the first time it became clear what was happening to Ronan Point," Webb said. "In high winds it was beginning to break up."[16] A new engineering appraisal determined that the building could never be made safe. Other system-built towers were also shedding panels and showing signs of falling apart. Webb predicted, "Sooner or later something will give. The question to be asked is whether we take these buildings down or gravity does it for us."[17]

Finally, in 1984, local authorities decided to demolish Ronan Point. Webb's concern was confirmed during the careful floor-by-floor demolition, which showed that the building's construction and workmanship were extremely shoddy. For example, joints in the walls that were supposed to be filled with mortar were instead filled with site rubbish. As a result, over the next decade hundreds of similar system-built high rises in Great Britain were condemned and demolished. Ronan Point forced both developers and public officials to focus more intently on safe building practices.

Location Is Everything

Ronan Point's design and construction flaws were exposed by an accidental gas explosion. British investigators determined, however, that a number of other loads, including high winds as well as uneven settlement of the foundation, also presented the potential for causing a disastrous progressive collapse. In other words, Ronan Point's location was a major determinant of dynamic and hidden loads the building was likely to face, and thus its overall safety.

Public officials and building designers juggle site demands all the time. For example, the likelihood of earthquakes in California has led it to develop one of the most comprehensive public approaches to seismic building safety in the world. Seaside regions on the East Coast have made progress in implementing designs to limit hurricane damage. The Federal Emergency Management Agency (FEMA) has recently suggested similar steps be taken in the country's "tornado alley," after the devastating 1999 Oklahoma City tornado. It partially or completely destroyed many homes and buildings that might have survived if they had had reinforced garage doors, stronger ground anchors, and sturdier roof connections. According to FEMA director James Lee Witt, speaking in March 2000 about the findings of a team of engineers and architects sent in to investigate the damage from the Oklahoma tornado outbreak, "They saw building failures that resulted from improper construction techniques, poor selection of construction materials, and ineffective detailing of connections of

▼ Better design and construction practices in tornado-prone areas may reduce home collapses like this one that occurred in Murfreesboro, Tennessee, in May 2003.

homes to foundations, floors to walls and walls to roofs." Witt added, "We cannot control the weather, but we can, in many cases, control its effects on people."[18] Witt and others called for houses and commercial buildings located in tornado-prone areas to be built to national wind standards.

Even in areas not threatened by such natural disasters, a building's overall strength, and thus its protection from collapse, is closely tied to whether the foundation rests upon a solid base. A major reason for the collapse of the Foggia apartment building was poor drainage of rainwater, resulting in constantly wet soil that gradually caused the foundation to become unstable.

From Wood to Steel

The Foggia apartment building may have been able to survive its poor soil base if its foundation had not been built with the cheap materials that investigators identified. The wood, stone or brick, reinforced concrete, and structural steel commonly used to construct buildings are another major factor in how they react to various potentially destructive forces. Each of these materials offers advantages and disadvantages relevant to building collapse.

Wood is a popular and versatile building material. It is not as strong as concrete or steel, but it is economical and if har-

THE PUSH AND PULL OF GRAVITY

Gravity is the bottom-line cause of every building collapse. Weaken or remove a building's structural supports—its columns, walls, beams, and girders—and gravity takes over, often with surprising suddenness. Gravity's constant pull toward the center of the earth, however, can also be used constructively, as when the force from an upper story promotes the strength of a foundation or the integrity of an arch.

Scientists have identified two basic actions that gravity has on building components: compression (a push downward that shortens material) and tension (a pull outward that stretches it). These actions directly affect choice of materials. Columns must be strong in compression, for example, while beams must resist both compression and tension. Stone and concrete are much stronger in compression than tension. Wood is more equal in how it resists pushing and pulling, which is why it is often used both as columns and beams. Structural steel is a popular building material because it is strong in both compression and tension.

vested sensibly is a sustainable resource. Drawbacks to the use of wood in buildings include its flammability and its susceptibility to damage by termites or other insects. Wood also needs to be protected from rotting and decay, which can be due either to moisture or to airborne fungi that get into the wood. A wooden building's overall strength depends not only on the type of wood but on how structural elements are joined together.

Masons have used stones, bricks, and other materials to make buildings for thousands of years. In fact the limestone-slab walls of temples, considered the oldest surviving buildings in the world, found on the Mediterranean islands of Malta and Gozo are still mostly intact after five thousand years. The strength of such simple masonry walls is due to the dead weight of overlying stones.

Concrete is typically a mixture of cement (a finely pulverized powder made up of silica, lime, and other compounds) and an aggregate such as sand and gravel. Adding water sets the cement and binds the mass into a strong material. Most people think of concrete as a modern invention. But the ancient Romans made use of concretelike materials in their buildings, roads, and aqueducts more than two thousand years ago. When the Roman Empire fell, circa A.D. 400, concrete was virtually abandoned as a building material until the early nineteenth century. Two innovations then boosted concrete's potential as a relatively durable and fire-resistant substance: the invention of portland cement (a particularly strong cement, derived from ground limestone and clay, that now dominates concrete production) and the use of round steel rods as embedded reinforcement.

Until the twentieth century, high-rises more than six stories tall had been built with brick walls, often supported by steel frames but also using much wood. Reinforced concrete was more economical and less of a fire hazard. Most tall buildings today are framed with structural steel, which is a human-made alloy containing iron and other metals. Walls of brick or other masonry cladding typically hang from the steel rather than act as structural support. Compared to reinforced concrete, steel is somewhat less resistant to fire, but steel is lighter and thus has been easier to use in skyscrapers. Steel is stronger than concrete against impact, although designers can adjust for this by making concrete columns bulky. Of course, this affects the building's overall weight.

Loads and materials are among the most important factors that determine how long a building will stand. Then again, buildings have been known to collapse even before they are finished, pointing to the importance of construction techniques in building safety.

When Buildings Fall on the Way Up

"I look at two or three buildings a year that collapse during construction," says engineer Steven Morris of Charlotte, North Carolina. Building construction is a risky time because structural elements usually are not all put into place at the same time. Thus, for example, the weight of a roof adds strength, through its downward force, to a correctly built wall. Until the roof is finished, however, walls are often held up with ad hoc, temporary bracing. A wind load that the finished

▼ Connecticut emergency personnel try to rescue construction workers at the site of the collapsed L'Ambiance Plaza.

building could handle easily might be enough to topple a partially built wall. This occurred in March 2000 at a strip shopping center under construction near Concord Mills, North Carolina. An inadequately braced masonry wall under construction collapsed from a gust of wind, killing two workers. According to Morris, "Unfortunately, you see that almost all the time. It's pretty common."[19]

Building authorities say that the incidence of construction failures in the United States has increased since the 1970s due to time-saving—but often risky—new building techniques. A tragic example of a speedy construction technique leading to disaster occurred on April 23, 1987, at L'Ambiance Plaza, a sixteen-story apartment building being built in Bridgeport, Connecticut. Workers were using a "lift-slab" construction technique whereby floors that were made from poured concrete at ground level were cured (allowed to harden) and then jacked into their final places along lifting rods. This could save time and money compared to hauling the concrete up to each floor and casting in place. The danger is that the building faces a much greater load during construction than after it is completed.

Construction workers had raised stacks of slabs to the ninth-floor level when something broke. "Suddenly a loud metallic bang rang out," Loretta Hall writes in *When Technology Fails*. "With an ominous rumble, cracks spread through the ninth-floor slab as through a shattering sheet of ice. The slab collapsed, pulling those above down with it. As the upper floors dropped, each lower floor crashed in succession."[20] The pancaking 320-ton concrete floors killed twenty-eight construction workers.

Modes of Failure

Exactly what triggered the L'Ambiance Plaza collapse is disputed, but a likely culprit is a failure in one of the connections or lifting collars on the upper slab. It was the second-worst construction accident in U.S. history, after the April 27, 1978, scaffolding collapse that killed fifty-one workers on a concrete cooling tower being built in Pleasants County, West Virginia. Not a single worker on the 170-foot tower at the time survived that disaster.

Two additional major construction accidents in the United States involved the pancaking collapse of concrete

IN PRAISE OF REDUNDANCY

The bane of essayists, redundancy is balm to structural engineers. In the building trade, redundancy means multiple approaches to structural support. Architects usually design redundancy into a structure so that it is capable of continuing to carry its loads if a single support mechanism fails. In effect, redundancy allows a load to follow alternate paths to the ground. If an arch fails, for example, a structural floor beam can pick up the additional load and prevent the building from collapsing. A building with adequate redundancy will provide clues, such as cracks, to its slow failure, rather than collapsing in a sudden and unforeseen manner.

In mid-January 1978, two major structures on the East Coast caved in: a seven-year-old, thirty-five-hundred-seat domed theater on the campus of C.W. Post College on Long Island, and the even larger, three-year-old, flat steel-roofed Hartford Civic Center Arena. No one was killed in either collapse, but if the Hartford incident had happened five hours earlier, the roof would have fallen on five thousand fans watching a basketball game. Heavy accumulations of snow and ice caused the collapses (and others that winter), but both of these buildings had insufficient redundancy in their designs that allowed the collapses.

▲ Only lucky timing prevented a major tragedy when the Hartford Civic Center collapsed.

floors. On March 2, 1973, a twenty-six-story apartment building under construction in Fairfax County, Virginia, collapsed when the temporary wood supports for a newly poured concrete floor at the twenty-second-floor level were removed too soon—according to some workers because the wood was needed elsewhere. The floor cracked and punched a hole through lower floors, claiming the lives of fourteen workers. On March 27, 1981, eleven workers were killed and two dozen injured during construction of the five-story Harbour Cay Condominiums in Cocoa Beach, Florida. An error in design, as well as faulty workmanship and inspection, led to a collapse during pouring of concrete for the roof slab.

The spate of tragic construction accidents the United States experienced during the 1970s and 1980s prompted government and construction-industry reforms that seem to have curtailed large-scale disasters. Plus, engineers are now more aware of the need to consider loads their buildings will face not only when finished but also during construction. Even so, floor and wall collapses due to faulty bracing, time-saving shortcuts, and lackadaisical inspections continue to claim the lives of construction workers, such as the four who died on October 30, 2003, when an Atlantic City, New Jersey, casino parking garage being built partially collapsed.

Nothing Lasts Forever

Relatively few buildings collapse before they are even completed, but all buildings begin the slow process of decay from the very moment of their ribbon cutting. Even the strongest structures in the world, the rock-solid pyramids of Egypt, are slowly crumbling: The Great Pyramid of Khufu (Cheops) outside Cairo has lost about 33 feet from its original height of 480 feet during the past four millennia, though mostly from shedding its limestone casing. (At this rate, its expected life span can still be projected out to more than fifty thousand years.) The slow, hidden load of water takes its toll, for example, as it gets into mortar and causes cracking through freeze-and-thaw cycles.

Unlike Egypt's pyramids, most buildings are not meant to be around forever. Cheap public housing like Ronan Point, for example, may have an estimated life span of barely more than half a century. Plenty of buildings have lasted for much longer, however, and engineers have developed techniques to watch for and repair weaknesses due to buildings' aging. Still, building collapses due to the effects of aging occur. The Civic Tower in the quaint northern Italian town of Pavia was built in 1060 to allow residents to see whether they were going to be attacked by their pesky neighbors, the Milanese. Few buildings last for a millennium and neither did the tower, which collapsed without warning on March 17, 1989, killing four. As the authors of *Why Buildings Fall Down: How Structures Fail* note:

> It disappeared in a cloud of red dust under the eyes of the terrified citizens crossing the cathedral square or walking along the narrow streets of the historic center. The roar of the collapse and the shaking of the ground were so horrific that the rumor spread instantly: "An earthquake has destroyed our cathedral."[21]

Actually it was not an earthquake at all but rather some risky design choices (for example, the structure was relatively narrow for its height) and centuries of questionable maintenance practices (new mortars used in repairs reacted chemically with old mortars to weaken the concrete walls) that helped to doom the tower. Perhaps just as important were the aging effects of air pollution and other hidden loads. The addition of a bell in the 1500s eventually took its toll, so to speak, by weakening the walls with sound wave vibrations every time it was rung. Street traffic in the twentieth century also exposed the aging structure to brick-cracking vibrations.

Maintenance and repair efforts can occasionally be much more immediately destructive, as was demonstrated recently at the Baikonur Cosmodrome, the Russian space launch site. Located in Kazakhstan, Baikonur features a number of 1960s-era spacecraft assembly and processing buildings. On May 12, 2002, eight construction workers were repairing the flat roof of one of the largest such facilities, Building 112, when the roof collapsed. All eight workers plunged two hundred feet to their deaths. The roof collapse wrecked a historic Soviet spacecraft, the *Buran* ("snowstorm"), a space-shuttle-like vehicle that in 1988 had made a single unmanned orbital flight. Russian and Kazakh investigators ultimately attributed the accident to the more than ten tons of rolled asphalt roofing that had been hauled to the roof to repair rain damage.

Dangerous New Lives for Old Buildings

Buildings that are successfully designed for one purpose may run into trouble as new owners, and varied uses, come and go. Modifications made without authorization are often a problem. In Egypt in 1992 two buildings collapsed killing thirty people, with the common factor being both had had an extra floor added illegally.

One of the more tragic recent building collapses took place on May 24, 2001, during a wedding reception party at the four-story Versailles Hall in West Jerusalem. Israeli Shlomi Srur and his family were among more than six hundred people attending. The mood was festive as scores of guests were doing a traditional foot-stomping Jewish dance, some with children in their arms. Srur got an ominous feeling, however, as he said to his son, "The floor is trembling here, something

▲ Tangled cables and rocket parts are open to the sky after a fatal roof failure at Russia's space launch center.

▲ Hundreds of Israelis fell in a deadly jumble of metal and concrete when a banquet hall floor gave way.

is wrong."[22] Minutes later the floor collapsed, hurling hundreds into a churning rubble.

According to Leah Hassin, a forty-nine-year-old guest who was dancing, "Suddenly I realized there was nothing under my feet. I was rolling in the air, as if I was parachuting but there was no parachute. Instead, I landed on my back and all I could see was a huge hole where the floor had been."[23] Hassin survived her fall but twenty-three people were killed, including Srur's wife and two of his sons, and three hundred were injured. The building had been built in 1986 for an industrial purpose and had been renovated (with at least one supporting column being removed) for use as a reception hall three months earlier. Investigators are also looking into the role of the building's cost-cutting construction method, known as Pal-Kal. Developed in the early 1980s, the technique used thin layers of cement between lightweight metal sheets for floors and ceilings. It was widely used in Israel before being banned in 1996.

Sampoong is another notable example of a collapse tied in part to change in purpose. The building had originally been designed as an office block. During construction, the owners decided to take advantage of South Korea's booming consumer economy and utilize the building as an upscale shopping complex. As *Collapse* author Phillip Wearne notes:

> The store had been built on a landfill site, and Woosung Construction, one of the country's largest construction firms, did the foundation and basement work before Sampoong's in-house contractors, Sampoong Construction, erected the superstructure. Woosung had apparently balked at making significant changes to the building plans, including the addition of a fifth floor. But in the hands of Sampoong's own construction company, the design changed even more radically.[24]

The design changes to accommodate an open-plan department store should have triggered structural adjustments. The building's owners decided to ignore this safety issue, and corrupt planning and inspection officials looked the other way. The combination of haste, greed, and ethical indifference led directly to the collapse and its horrific toll of deaths and injuries.

The Immediate Concern

The various reasons for the Sampoong collapse became apparent as investigators interviewed survivors and combed through the physical evidence. Finding out exactly what happened is always a top priority, but rescue is even more of an immediate concern. After a collapse has happened, injured survivors often are pinned under the rubble, which remains unstable and hazardous to survivors and rescuers alike.

CHAPTER THREE

Rescue: Danger and Urgency

On September 11, 2001, thousands of New York City firefighters, police officers, and medical workers responded to the fast-developing emergency that took place when terrorists crashed airliners into the two World Trade Center towers. Two hundred units of firefighting companies from all over the city sent trucks and equipment. Senior fire department officials set up a command post near the fire control panels in the first-floor lobby of WTC-1, the first building hit. Some five hundred firefighters began the arduous task of lugging tons of equipment up the eighty floors to try to fight the raging fires. The oxygen tanks, hoses, axes, and other tools burdened many with more than sixty pounds of extra weight.

Policemen on the ground and in the building lobbies helped to clear the surrounding area and evacuate occupants. Paramedics and other emergency medical workers treated hundreds of people who poured out of the two buildings, including many who were badly burned. Other victims were injured on the ground from falling debris.

More than 400 of these heroic public servants, predominantly firefighters, were killed when the two massive skyscrapers collapsed. A 2003 study by federal fire researchers determined that an additional 180 firefighters were killed in structural collapses between 1979 and 2002. This tragic loss of life among first responders is a graphic illustration of the extreme dangers posed by building collapses.

Challenges on the Ground

Rescue efforts at the scene of a collapsed building face three major challenges, the first and most obvious one being the extremely dangerous conditions. Whether a building has been damaged by structural failure, explosion, or earthquake, the collapse area is likely to be chaotic and unpredictable. Huge pieces of shifting concrete can crush, explosive gas can kill, shards of broken glass can cut, and live wires can electrocute. The fire that burned within the WTC rubble for three months was the longest-burning structural fire in history. Even minor hazards can be extremely dangerous after a structural collapse, notes the United Kingdom Fire Services Search & Rescue Team:

> For example, emergency lights become flesh-devouring acid pools, yet only appearing as wet spots on walls. The severe dust contains every disease that has been safely buried for the past few hundred years just waiting to find a nice warm moist home in your lungs. Water and sewage systems, electrical wires, and hazardous materials, among others, may pose danger.[25]

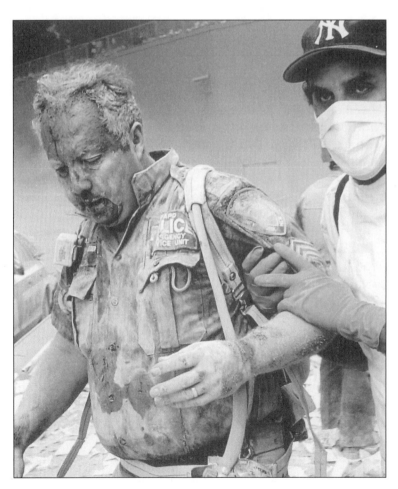

◄ A Port Authority policeman is led away after suffering injuries during the collapse of WTC-2.

The second major challenge that rescuers face is the need for speedy action. The people who are buried alive within this nightmare scene often have serious injuries. Most will die if not rescued within the first few hours of a building collapse. Studies done on survivors of earthquake-caused building collapses have found that the vast majority are rescued within the first twenty-four hours.

The third major challenge relates to the difficulty of simply finding and removing victims. People can be buried under so much rubble they cannot be seen or heard. Safely moving tons of rubble to reach these people can require strength and stamina, and often demands special tools and skills.

With trained and untrained rescue workers working urgently in dangerous conditions, it is not surprising that injuries and deaths among search-and-rescue teams are common—135 would-be rescuers were killed after the Mexico City earthquake of 1985.

First to Arrive: Friends and Neighbors

Damage to buildings after the Mexico City earthquake was extensive. A twenty-one-story steel-frame office building collapsed as well as a number of mid-rise concrete buildings. Thousands of smaller buildings over a ten-square-mile area were also affected by the quake and a jarring aftershock. Many of the rescuers who were the first on the scene at the Mexico City disaster were ordinary citizens—relatives, friends, and neighbors who survived the quake and quickly pitched in to help save those in trouble. Such impromptu volunteers often play a major role in the immediate aftermath of a multiple-building-collapse scene because an earthquake or other natural disaster typically disrupts communications, clogs streets, and spreads emergency responders thin.

The heroic rescue efforts of ordinary citizens are often spurred by the need to save family members and friends. Those who survive a disaster are also likely to know who is missing and where they were last seen, which can make it easier to find victims. According to the authors of a study of a massive gasoline explosion in the Mexican city of Guadalajara in April 1992 that destroyed or collapsed more than one thousand buildings in a neighborhood area, "Chances of people surviving the blast were directly proportional to the presence among searchers of a person or persons who cared for the victim and who knew the victim's likely location."[26]

◄ Citizen rescuers pull a victim out of the rubble of a house collapsed by an earthquake in Turkey in August 1999.

One of the most successful rescuers after the Mexico City earthquake was a small, athletic man who earned the nickname "the flea" by scrambling into tight spots to help save many seemingly doomed people. The selfless actions of volunteers like him have historically saved more lives than have the actions of professional rescuers. This was especially evident in Mexico City, where volunteers saved some five hundred people within the first twenty-four hours, compared to another hundred rescued over the next ten days. A 1989 study found that 97 percent of the injured victims of a 1980 earthquake in Italy were rescued with bare hands, shovels, and ladders. Search-and-rescue workers refer to the first hour after a building collapse as the "golden hour," since the odds of finding survivors shrink so rapidly with time.

As disaster researchers noted in a report on lessons learned from the Kobe earthquake, "Consistent with patterns observed in other disasters worldwide, most search and rescue was undertaken by community residents; officially-designated rescue agencies such as fire departments and [Japan's national] Self Defense Forces were responsible for recovering at most one-quarter of those trapped in collapsed structures."[27]

Search and Rescue Turns Pro

The heroic actions of volunteers often come at the price of further tragedy, as would-be rescuers fall, get burned, or are killed by shifting rubble. The high death toll among volunteer rescuers in Mexico City was mainly due to building and rubble collapses, although a number of the fatalities occurred when water mains flooded basements under collapsed buildings, drowning rescuers. The U.S. Occupational Safety and Health Administration has estimated that an untrained rescuer has at least a fifty-fifty chance of getting killed by entering a collapsed building.

The arrival of civil authorities and professional rescuers can at times lead to conflicts as they take over from ordinary citizens. When the hijacked airliner hit the Pentagon on September 11, 2001, army colonel Ted Anderson was in the building. In the immediate aftermath he and others helped a number of injured people to safety, but were soon forced to the sidelines. According to Anderson:

▼ Firefighters battle smoke and flames at the section of the Pentagon struck by a hijacked airliner on September 11, 2001.

We were screaming at the firemen, "there are people in that corridor, please let us go get them. They're Army. We're Army." There were generals there with us. We said we would take responsibility for our own welfare. But they couldn't allow that to happen. . . . They held us back. There were hundreds of people standing around me, and it occurred to

BUILDING COLLAPSE RESCUE 101

In addition to building collapse rescue being taught in federal facilities and engineering schools, specialized field classes and courses are now offered in a number of locales. For example, in November 1999 construction and emergency specialists converged on Charlottesville, Virginia, to conduct a thirty-hour training course in concrete building collapse rescue. Participants learned how to use concrete-cutting chain saws within tight confines and how to build timber cribbing to raise a heavy concrete slab. "Breaching and breaking" exercises using heavy hydraulic jackhammers demonstrated how difficult it can be to break through a concrete floor or wall. Students were also presented with the tough challenge of moving a four-by-four-foot solid block of concrete through an obstacle course using only simple tools like levers and rollers. The ancient Egyptians might have passed this test—they pioneered various large-block-moving techniques while building their pyramids.

me later that we must have appeared like protestors, the way they were holding us back. . . . Of course, the firefighters were saving our lives, by not allowing us in.[28]

Within recent decades there has been an increased focus on search-and-rescue training, to get professional care to victims more quickly and to prevent rescue-related deaths. In a number of countries, trained rescue personnel with specialized equipment now routinely respond to building collapses. In the United States, the NASA Ames Research Center in Moffett Field, California, has developed an extensive emergency response and recovery training and testing facility. Its Collapsed Structure Rescue Training Site features a large concrete rubble pile with built-in voids and a simulated collapsed building. Since 1992 the center has offered an annual, six-day collapsed structure rescue class that provides training in topics such as tools and techniques for lifting, moving, and supporting heavy objects within a confined space, and construction of temporary shoring to prevent further collapse.

Organized teams at a building collapse typically work systematically to cover every square foot of a site. Tape and markers may be used to set up a visible grid, so rescuers can spread out and keep track of their movements. Working down from the top of the rubble pile, rescuers listen for injured persons and search for voids that they can enter and explore. Professionals may have more training and equipment than the first-on-the-site citizens, but they all face the same dangers and challenges. Rappelling down a rope into a dark void is inherently hazardous. Deaths and injuries among professional emergency crews are rare but not unheard of.

An Emergency Role for Engineers

The April 1995 bombing of the Murrah Federal Building in Oklahoma City was a difficult rescue, in part because of the complex condition of the partially collapsed building. The search-and-rescue operation was one of the first times that engineers played a major role. FEMA and the Oklahoma City Fire Department deployed more than three dozen "rescue engineers" to evaluate the partially crumbled structure, monitor rubble movement, and make sure the rescue operation was safe and effective. Among the special tools rescue engineers may use are devices for measuring horizontal and vertical angles, the width of cracks, and changes in slope. As rescue engineer specialist Solveig Thorvald points out,

> The engineer's role is not to give commands but to give advice on critical structural issues. The list of concerns is long, including the stability of the remaining structure and the rubble, how the operations of rubble removal will affect the stability of the remaining structure, how to shore up the structure, determining the level of risk for those inside, monitoring the building for movement, determining the level of risk from hanging hazards, and how to quickly mitigate hazards.[29]

How easy or difficult it is to extract a person who has been trapped in a collapsed building is greatly influenced by the type of building and exactly how it collapsed. Engineers' knowledge of building structure can therefore play a major role in determining the best way to proceed with the rescue. In some instances engineers have had to warn rescuers that a structure is dangerously unstable or too unsafe to enter. Conflicts between engineers, who are mainly concerned with rescuer safety, and rescue workers, who are primarily focused on saving victims, may have to be resolved by rescue team leaders.

See Me, Hear Me

Rescuers use a number of methods and technologies to try to locate survivors. Rescuers have traditionally shut down all

▲ Engineers help to direct the work of rescue crews and crane operators at Oklahoma City's partially collapsed Murrah Federal Building.

work, especially the noisy bulldozers, cranes, and jackhammers, at a collapse site every hour or so to quietly listen for calls for help. Survivors too weak to call out have been known to rap on pipes or make other sounds to try to draw attention to themselves. After the Guadalajara gasoline explosion, a man and his two nephews trapped near each other in their collapsed house coordinated their screams for help at a count of three to successfully attract the attention of rescuers. A few of the firefighters rescued from the World Trade Center debris contacted emergency officials with cell phones or radios.

At the site of the collapsed WTC towers, Penn State acoustics researchers tested a promising rescue technology: dropping wireless, expendable microphones into the rubble. By the date of the test (September 18, 2001), it was clear that ground zero likely held no further survivors, but the test confirmed that the small but toughly built microphones can be put into areas that are still potentially hot or unstable. There they can amplify the sounds of survivors calling out for help, sounds that are often difficult to hear on top of the rubble. "These results support the strategy of lowering microphones into collapsed structures in addition to listening for survivor signals from the surface. Placing the microphone in voids in the collapsed structure reduces much of the surface-produced airborne noise,"[30] the Penn State researchers concluded.

▲ Ground zero search-
and-rescue teams
included specially
trained dogs.

In recent years rescuers have also begun to use high-tech viewing devices during building rescues. Tiny, fiber-optic video cameras can be lowered into the debris to peer around corners and under slabs. Infrared cameras that pick up images of heat can lead rescuers to trapped survivors. Cameras have also successfully been mounted on remote-controlled robots, and some researchers have even suggested putting them on specially trained rats.

Most search-and-rescue people, it must be admitted, consider loosing rats upon a building collapse site to be particularly misguided. Dogs, on the other hand, have often been successfully used at building collapses because of their ability to sniff out survivors.

Heavy Lifters and Cutters Needed

Whether humans, machines, or animals locate a collapse survivor, rescuers must then use great care to prevent further collapse in the area and to safely extricate the person. "It's like undoing a 3-D jigsaw puzzle," says British fire expert Colin Williams. "You have got to be very careful you don't bring debris down on the heads of people who might still be alive."[31] The well-intentioned but sometimes uninformed actions of volunteers can be especially worrisome in this regard. According to researchers who investigated the Guadalajara search and rescue, "We learned of one instance in which volunteers climbed a pile of rubble in which a woman was trapped. Their collective weight collapsed the internal cavity that had protected her, killing her."[32]

The best way to rescue someone trapped in building collapse debris, according to paramedic and building collapse expert Clark Staten, involves "carefully lifting the debris from above the victim and continually 'shoring' the sides of the entrance hole or excavation to ensure against additional collapse." He adds:

As many as one-third of all building collapse victims, that are rescued, are found in spaces created by the way that building materials generally fall. Most of the collapse configurations that occur (lean-to, A-frame, tent, pancake) create "voids" in which people may be trapped and remain alive. [Horizontal] movement of debris will normally further collapse the sides of these "protective spaces" and can result in additional deaths of those that might have been rescued.[33]

Debris sometimes can be removed by hand or by using small tools, but in many cases specialized materials and equipment are crucial. These include gas-powered saws, acetylene torches, pry axes and bars, pneumatic jackhammers, electric drills, and other powerful tools for breaking through concrete and cutting rebar. Overhead cranes may be called in to lift heavy materials. A popular tool among emergency teams that may have to make confined space rescues at a

 ROBOTS TO THE RESCUE

At the WTC, search teams used a dozen football-sized robots for the first time in a building collapse. The robots were able to fit into spaces too small, or too dangerous, for human rescuers. Although the $30,000 machines did not find any survivors, the experience gained using them has led to more advanced second-generation models. According to Robin Murphy, director of the University of South Florida–based Center for Robot-Assisted Search and Rescue, researchers are developing technology "that we hope will enable the robot to detect whether a victim is alive, but unconscious, and return radio signals reporting vital life signs. We are also organizing an exploratory project to evaluate what it takes to have the robots carry in and control airbags to shore up a collapsed structure."

► Spades and sledgehammers were among the tools that Brazilian rescue workers used to search for survivors of a September 2002 building collapse in Rio de Janeiro.

building collapse is the Hurst Jaws of Life spreading and cutting tool, made by Hale Products of Conshohocken, Pennsylvania. It is lightweight but powerful enough to generate fifteen tons of cutting force.

Rescuers have also helped to develop additional equipment for use in shoring up areas of the collapse. The usual methods include constructing temporary bracing by nailing together two-by-fours, stacking timber beams to form a cribbing framework, and setting up adjustable steel props. A high-tech alternative is to use inflatable, high-pressure air bags that have been specially designed for rescues. Paratech of Frankfort, Illinois, offers an array of such rectangular, fiber-reinforced air bags, including some that can be inserted in a one-inch space but are tough enough when inflated (using an air compressor, for example) to lift or shift a seventy-ton concrete slab.

Medical Trauma

As difficult as finding a building collapse survivor can be, saving the person's life faces additional hurdles. Rescuers may use specialized ropes, slings, and stretchers to retrieve injured survivors. Before moving victims, medical personnel may need to treat the burns, broken bones, and cuts inflicted by the deadly shower of glass, concrete, and wood. Loss of blood and bodily fluids, internal injuries, or rubble on the neck or chest that restricts breathing can leave survivors unconscious, in shock, and on the verge of death. Victims who have had large muscle groups, such as the upper legs, subjected to crushing pressure for an hour or longer may require specialized care as soon as the pressure is released, due to bodily reactions that can be life-threatening. What doctors call "crush injury syndrome" may also necessitate long-term treatment with kidney dialysis. One estimate is that 8,000 of the more than 160,000 people injured in the 1976 Tangshan, China, earthquake suffered crush injury syndrome.

◄ A Lebanese woman screams in pain as she is pulled from the rubble of an apartment block that collapsed near Beirut in November 2000.

Even among victims who have not been badly injured, pneumonia or other lung conditions may develop from inhaling microscopic particles suspended in the clouds of dust generated during a collapse. Toxic materials from concrete, asbestos insulation, office equipment, and other sources can accumulate in the tiny air sacs of the lungs and cause either acute ailments or long-term concerns such as cancer. After the collapse of the two WTC towers, federal officials downplayed the adverse health effects from the massive toxic dust clouds, as well as from the smoke due to the persistent fires. Over the next year, however, many ground zero rescue workers and residents of lower Manhattan began to suffer from various respiratory conditions, including "World Trade Center cough." The long-term health threat has underscored the need for rescue workers at building collapse sites to be provided with respirators to protect them from airborne pollutants.

TREATING CRUSH INJURY SYNDROME

During World War I doctors were mystified when people who were pulled from the rubble of bombed buildings would die shortly after being rescued, even though they had only seemingly minor injuries. Within recent decades medical researchers have tied such deaths to the sudden changes in bodily chemistry that accompany release from entrapment. According to Eric Noji, who was the UN's chief medical officer in Turkey after its destructive August 1999 earthquake, "Just as the rescuers pull that last piece of concrete or slab of plaster off the person's leg or arm, it's like taking a tourniquet off." The release of the compressing force may cause sudden blood loss. Potassium that has built up in muscle tissue is another major concern, since it can enter the bloodstream and quickly interfere with heart function. Search-and-rescue physicians like Noji may need to immediately inject a crush injury victim with a special intravenous solution. People who survive crush injuries often require long recovery periods and may end up permanently disabled.

Until Hope Is Exhausted

The possibility that someone remains buried alive is why most rescue attempts continue until every reasonable hope has been exhausted. The vast majority of collapse survivors are found within the first twenty-four hours but remarkable cases occur. For example, in 1992 Turkish rescuers pulled a twenty-two-year-old nurse from beneath a building eight days after it collapsed during an earthquake. She said that for several days after the collapse, she had been talking with two friends who were also buried, until she "didn't hear them anymore."[34] A part-time fitness instructor was rescued from the basement of a Hyatt hotel fourteen days after a 1990 earthquake in the Philippines buried him in debris.

◄ Victims can sometimes survive for days under a collapsed building, like this young girl pulled from the rubble in Turkey one hundred hours after the collapse.

Most such long-term survivors are young people in good health. Access to water during their entrapment is crucial—people can survive without food for weeks or even months but for only a matter of days without water. Frequent rain that filtered through the rubble saved a number of those trapped in Sampoong, where three young store employees managed to survive for more than a week in separate parts of the collapse site. The most remarkable of these was Park Seung-Hyun, who was rescued an astonishing sixteen days after the collapse.

Given the possibility that victims might still be alive even two weeks after a building collapse, when to stop a rescue attempt and shift efforts to site clearing is often a difficult decision. A rule of thumb offered by Staten is that it is not over until every potential building occupant is accounted for, or the site is cleared of debris. How that gets implemented can be tricky, especially when destruction is widespread, as after an earthquake. Relatives of still-lost victims have been known to block advancing bulldozers.

After September 11, 2001, officials treated the World Trade Center site as a rescue scene for seventeen days even though not a single survivor was found more than twenty-six

MIRACLE AT SAMPOONG

Nineteen-year-old Park Seung-Hyun was working in a clothing department on the second floor of Sampoong when the building suddenly began to collapse. She ran for an exit but was hit in the head and knocked out by a heavy chunk of ceiling debris. Seung-Hyun awoke to find herself trapped in a tiny void on the building's second basement level, under tons of rubble. She managed to survive by drinking rainwater and refusing to give up. "I slept, woke up, slept, woke up tens of times," she says in Phillip Wearne's *Collapse: When Buildings Fall Down*. The darkness and heat were suffocating, and the cramped space she was trapped in kept shrinking ever more alarmingly as rescue work went on over-

head. Without enough room to even turn around, she despaired that anyone would ever hear her feeble banging on the broken concrete.

Eventually, a heavy equipment operator clearing debris somehow heard her soft moans. She later recalled, "I heard someone say, 'There is someone down there!' and I heard digging right above where I was. I saw his face and my only thought was I was going to live. I could finally leave this darkness." Too weak and injured to walk, Seung-Hyun was removed by stretcher and transported to a hospital, though she soon recovered from her ordeal. Her astonished mother spoke for all when she said, "It's a miracle."

hours after the collapse. For months more the "rescue" at the WTC was extended to include recovery of remains of missing persons—fewer than three hundred intact bodies but almost twenty thousand body parts, some identified only by DNA. The WTC collapse site was unusual in that regard, but it was typical in another: Even while the rescue was ongoing, building collapse investigators had begun to comb the scene for clues to determine exactly how and why the buildings fell.

CHAPTER FOUR

Challenging Investigations

O n July 17, 1981, a huge crowd of Friday night revelers had gathered inside the elegant Hyatt Regency hotel in Kansas City, Missouri. Like a number of other newly built Hyatt hotels, this one had a dramatic interior atrium that enclosed four stories under a steel and glass roof. With its adjoining restaurants and bars, the atrium space had become one of the city's most popular entertainment venues. By seven o'clock, an estimated sixteen hundred people had shown up for the night's tea dance with live music.

Scores of the partygoers were watching the throng of dancers on the lobby floor from a second-story skywalk, in effect a hanging sidewalk along the west side of the atrium that connected two wings of the building. Even more couples were on the fourth-floor skywalk directly above (the third-floor skywalk was offset from the other two). A bar was set up underneath the second-story skywalk. Spirits were high as the Steve Miller Orchestra broke into a rendition of Duke Ellington's jazz tune "Satin Doll."

Suddenly, a loud screeching sound stunned the crowd into silence and focused attention on the second- and fourth-story skywalks. The concrete, glass, and steel structures pulled loose from their supports, sagged, and then collapsed with a sickening roar into the atrium. People and debris crashed to the lobby floor in a deadly tumult. "People were screaming," note the authors of *Why Buildings Fall Down.* "The west glass wall adjacent to the walkways shattered, sending shards flying over 100 feet . . . pipes broken by the falling walkways sent jets of water spraying the atrium floor. It was a nightmare the survivors would never forget."[35]

▲ Investigators faced a scene of scattered wreckage after the Hyatt Regency skywalk disaster.

Figuring Out What Went Wrong

The shocking skywalk failure killed 114 people and injured 200 more, making it the worst structural failure in U.S. history. Even as rescue workers rushed to the scene of the Hyatt Regency, forces were being mobilized to determine how such a disaster could have happened. City officials, hotel representatives, the general contractor that built the hotel, insurance agents, victims' lawyers, and reporters had a keen interest in determining what had happened and who was at fault.

The various building collapse investigators who flocked to the Hyatt Regency faced some of the same basic challenges as did the rescuers. These included a potentially dangerous accident scene and the need to sort through tons of rubble to find what they were looking for—not victims to rescue but clues to ponder. Hazardous conditions can lead to accidents and fatalities. In January 1999, for example, a career fire and building collapse investigator with the Syracuse, New York, fire department was looking for clues in the attic of a partially burned house. The sudden collapse of the building's brick chimney killed him. Another major challenge is analyzing the clues and reconstructing exactly what happened. Special scientific skills and knowledge are required to unravel something as complex as a building collapse, and the professionals with this unique background are now known as forensic engineers.

Forensic engineering as a field has grown in leaps and bounds in recent years. Structural disasters are common enough that the profession of failure analysis seems recession proof. Designers are constantly exploring the edges of structural feasibility, builders skimp on material and labor to keep construction budgets tight, and budget-conscious local jurisdictions trim building inspection services to a minimum. Since the 1970s, according to the authoritative text *Forensic Engineering: Environmental Case Histories for Civil Engineers and Geologists,* there has been "a veritable explosion" of forensic work involving all branches of engineering. "Many civil engineers and geologists," authors Gerard Shuirman and James Slosson note, "spend most of their professional time doing forensic work; some devote all of their time to it."[36]

Forensic engineering has developed rapidly in response not only to bridge and building failures but also to faulty consumer products. At the prominent Los Angeles–based firm Exponent, forensic engineer Lisa Shusto-Borghi says that failure analysis is "the Sherlock Holmes work of engineering—figuring out what went wrong."[37] Forensic engineers use scientific knowledge to solve engineering problems, often turning to microscopes, X-ray machines, and other high-tech tools to examine cracks or identify the composition of a building material. The profession now has numerous firms and practitioners, its

EXPERTS PROBE OKLAHOMA CITY

Perhaps the most prominent American expert in building collapses is forensic engineer W. Gene Corley, who led the investigations into the collapse of the Murrah Federal Building in Oklahoma City and the WTC. To help unravel the cause of the Oklahoma City collapse, his team visited the site, collected samples of structural components, took photographs, and reviewed construction documents. It organized tests of materials taken from the site, such as concrete and reinforcing bars, to determine the physical properties of materials used in the building. Investigators also measured the size of the bomb crater and analyzed explosion evidence to estimate the loads imposed on the building.

own scientific journals, and advanced-level college courses in the topic. When the Hyatt Regency skywalk collapsed, forensic engineers were called upon to review the design, materials, and construction methods.

Diverse Investigative Skills Needed

Although forensic engineers are key players in any building collapse investigation, various other experts often play major roles, including architects, materials scientists, geologists, building code officials, and academics. For the WTC investigation, the preeminent professional organization the American Society of Civil Engineers (ASCE) and FEMA partnered to form a twenty-five-person team with experts on tall-building design, metallurgy, fire engineering, and blast effects. Diverse skills are needed because investigations look into every aspect of a building's design, construction, and use for insights into what went wrong.

Among investigators' initial tasks are to observe and survey the disaster site and to interview eyewitnesses, technical experts, survivors, and first responders. Investigators also

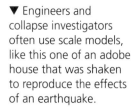

▼ Engineers and collapse investigators often use scale models, like this one of an adobe house that was shaken to reproduce the effects of an earthquake.

NIST TAKES OVER

In the United States, the early stages of the WTC investigation prompted harsh criticism from some lawmakers. They noted that various government agencies involved often had conflicting agendas. The FBI, for example, was concerned with a criminal investigation, and the National Institute of Standards and Technology (NIST) with identifying how and why the buildings fell. One result was that criminal investigators took pieces of steel and other potential clues from the sites before structural experts could examine them. Investigators also argued over jurisdiction and access to blueprints.

The investigation was widely perceived to be so flawed that in 2002 federal lawmakers passed, and President George W. Bush signed, a law that changed how the federal government responds to major building collapses. NIST, a nonregulatory agency of the Commerce Department, is now assigned the job of investigating building failures that cause substantial loss of life. It is supposed to function much like the federal government's National Transportation Safety Board, which investigates airplane crashes, railroad accidents, and shipwrecks.

view any relevant photos or videos and pore over documents, ranging from blueprints to inspection reports, to determine what the building was like just before the structural failure. Experts collect and scrutinize debris, carefully mapping its depth and location. "You excavate down through the layers and you can go back through time, back through the sequence of failure,"[38] structural engineer John Osteraas says in *Collapse*. Such diligence is necessary to evaluate disaster scenarios and to calculate how the building's ability to carry various loads had been compromised.

Clues in the Rubble

In the Hyatt Regency case, investigators had an almost ideal disaster scene—indoors, easily roped off from the public, numerous surviving witnesses, and limited amounts of debris to sift through for clues. At the outset a number of possible causes were kept in mind, chief among them simple overloading of the walkways. Should the walkways have held the number of people crammed onto them?

It turned out that evidence supplied by a local television crew filming the dance helped to prove overloading was not the cause. Footage showed a total of sixty-three people on the

▲ Skywalk investigators initially suspected resonance, the cumulative movement that famously shook apart the Tacoma Narrows Bridge in 1940.

second- and fourth-story walkways. Engineers calculated that the peoples' weight, approximately ten thousand pounds, was a fraction of the walkways' presumed carrying capacity—each should have held more than seventy thousand pounds. "The catwalks were designed to hold people shoulder to shoulder—as many as you can jam on there,"[39] Hyatt Hotels president Pat Foley told the *New York Times*.

Another possibility was that the movement of the people on the walkways had induced a dangerous resonance. The accident occurred during a dance, and rhythmic steps could have set up a fatal wave action. Scientists have been acutely aware of the potential for small movements to have cumulative effects ever since Washington State's Tacoma Narrows Bridge shook itself apart in a forty-two-mile-per-hour wind on November 7, 1940. Film of the suspension bridge's roadbed violently rippling and then plunging into Puget

Sound has become a staple of television disaster shows. In Kansas City, although survivors reported that the walkways were undulating to the rhythm of dancers, the movement was not dramatic and engineers were able to discount resonance as a factor in the collapse.

Within a day, investigators instead began to focus on potential defects in the hanger rods that had been used to suspend the walkways. The hotel's original design called for the two walkways to be suspended from a series of single steel rods. An analogy is two people hanging, one above the other, from the same rope. This design would have held the walkways, although it turned out that even this design did not satisfy Kansas City Building Code provisions. The original design, however, was vague on crucial details and seemed to pose tricky problems in execution for the building's contractors.

A Deadly Redesign

The contractors therefore decided to improvise on the site, a not uncommon occurrence in any major project. The company charged with fabricating the skywalk's steel components devised a new method for hanging the structure. The fabricators then submitted the plan to the project's architects as well as its structural engineers, who reviewed and approved it. The revised design called for hanging the upper walkway from one set of rods and the lower walkway from a second set of rods descending from the upper walkway. The analogy was now one person hanging from a rope, with a second person hanging from his leg. Even if the rope is strong, the top person's grip is under a lot of additional strain. The load on it, in fact, is double that of the original design.

The architects, contractors, fabricators, and structural engineers all failed to recognize the hazard from putting so much more pressure on the connecting points, where the rods were attached to the box girders supporting the fourth-floor walkway. The simple washers and nuts that were sufficient for the first design were dangerously inadequate to the new design, which at the very least needed sturdy plates installed where the rods held the walkways. Lacking this means of distributing the load, the force exerted on the welded beam at the site of the small washers and nuts was excessive—so much so that the fourth-floor walkway was barely capable of supporting its own weight, much less its weight plus scores of people.

A Fatal Design Change at the Hyatt Regency

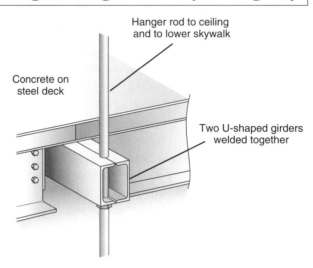

Hanger rod to ceiling and to lower skywalk

Concrete on steel deck

Two U-shaped girders welded together

The intitial design was for both skywalks to hang from a single rod anchored in the ceiling.

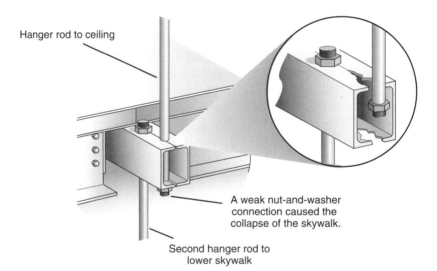

Hanger rod to ceiling

A weak nut-and-washer connection caused the collapse of the skywalk.

Second hanger rod to lower skywalk

The flawed actual construction attached the lower skywalk to a second hanger rod.
The added strain allowed a nut and washer on one rod to pull through the weld in a girder,
causing the collapse of both skywalks.

Investigators determined that the combined live and dead load at one connecting point on the fourth-floor walkway opened a weld in a box girder, letting that section of the walkway slide past the washer and nut connection. This set off a chain reaction of connection failures on the fourth-floor skywalk, leading to its sudden collapse. It hit the second-floor walkway on the way down, killing many of the people on the two walkways as well as others on the crowded lobby floor.

Inside the High-Tech Labs

After on-scene investigators gather their evidence, they make use of various high-tech labs at government agencies, universities, and companies around the world to identify and test debris and other materials. Advanced machines and technologies allow scientists to analyze the properties of metals and concrete, build structural replicas to test for accidents, and measure the resistance of materials to crack or burn. Building collapse investigators may use machines that stretch or compress materials, spectrometers that analyze chemical components, or microscopes that reveal molecular structures to try to determine how and why a building failed.

At the NIST's Building and Fire Research Lab (BFRL) in Gaithersburg, Maryland, specialized facilities that may be useful in collapse investigations include a computer-controlled wind tunnel and a test apparatus capable of applying loads simultaneously in three directions. There is also a building-stone test wall that is now almost sixty years old and beginning to yield valuable data on the effects of weathering on different types of stones. The high-tech federal facilities are often rented out to industry researchers and academics.

▼ Building collapse expert Matthys Levy explains a computer-generated picture of a plane crashing into WTC-1, during the investigation into why the towers collapsed.

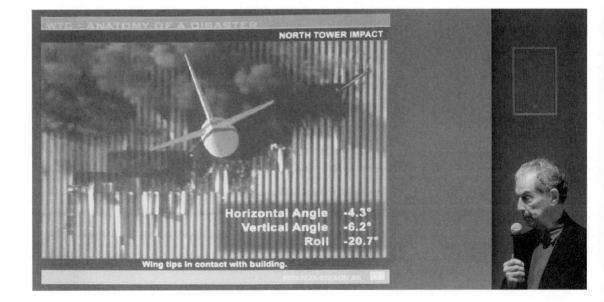

WTC : ANATOMY OF A DISASTER

NORTH TOWER IMPACT

Horizontal Angle   -4.3°
Vertical Angle   -6.2°
Roll   -20.7°

Wing tips in contact with building.

A COLOSSAL COLUMN CRUSHER

Perhaps the BFRL's most impressive piece of equipment is a hydraulically operated "universal testing machine" that is the largest such device in the world. This massive, high-tech apparatus can twist and compress concrete columns up to five feet in diameter to test how they would perform under duress. Researchers say that it is amazing to watch this monster crunch a thick, thirty-foot-high building column. The compressive force the machine can apply exceeds 12 million pounds. Such tools can play a useful role in simulating the two-dimensional, horizontal/vertical forces that structural building components may face during an earthquake.

Building collapse investigators may also develop sophisticated computer models. For example, researchers have recently discovered new ways to use lasers to map the interior and exterior of weak or damaged buildings. The data is fed into a computer capable of creating high-resolution, three-dimensional images of the building, showing areas under excessive load or with tiny displacements and cracks.

Digging for Root Causes

Determining the immediate physical cause for a building collapse is often only the initial stage of a full-scale investigation. It can be just as important to identify broader procedures and policies that somehow failed to recognize the problem and prevent the disaster. For example, in the Hyatt Regency case, the walkways fell because of poorly designed, insufficiently reinforced, and improperly used hanger rods. But investigators also determined that the architects should have recognized the practical difficulties of their original design; the structural engineer who approved the revised design should have noticed the dangerous new way the load was being borne; and local inspectors should have caught and questioned both the out-of-code original design and the fatal design change. The many resulting lawsuits spread blame far and wide, as the authors of *Construction Disasters* note:

> In various court documents the steel fabricator has said the structural engineer made the change, the engineer said it was the fabricator's idea, the contractor has blamed the engineer and the architectural joint venture, the construc-

tion manager has blamed the contractor or steel fabricator, and the architects have blamed the engineer or steel fabricator or both.[40]

The existence of such multiple causes for major disasters is more the rule than the exception. The Hyatt Regency investigators may have been especially aware of this fact because of another well-publicized structural failure, the Kemper Arena roof collapse, that had happened in Kansas City barely two years earlier. Its cause was also clearly traced to an interplay of human and mechanical factors.

Minor Details, Multiple Causes

In 1979 the Kemper Arena was a five-year-old, seventeen-thousand-seat arena that had received a coveted architectural award and held a Republican Party national convention. The building's almost-square flat roof, a football-field long and wide, was held up by an innovative design featuring three gigantic, space-frame trusses. Extending over the roof, the steel trusses were anchored into the ground and bolted to the structure. Only a few maintenance and security workers were in the arena on the night of July 4, 1979, when a severe rainstorm deposited four inches of rain on the building's roof. Suddenly about one-third of the roof gave way, sending the arena's massive hanging scoreboard crashing to the floor amid tons of water and debris.

▼ Kansas City's Kemper Arena suffered an embarrassing roof failure that investigators eventually tied to multiple causes.

No one was injured, but the Kemper Arena failure was an embarrassing blow to the architectural and building community. The roof should have been able to sustain a much heavier load than it did. Investigators determined that a number of design, construction, and weather factors contributed to the collapse. The eight drains on the roof were too small to handle the sudden deluge. High winds pushed the accumulating rainwater to one side of the building, where it built up to nine inches deep. The bolts connecting the trusses to the roof had been weakened over time by wind-induced rocking, and some of the bolts had not been sufficiently tightened during construction. The innovative use of trusses in the roof design was not faulty—the building's damaged roof was later reconstructed using the same basic structure. Rather, designers and builders had paid insufficient attention to seemingly minor details, like the number of drains and the reliability of bolts, that ultimately combined with an unusual storm to cause the roof to fail.

Investigators' Verdict on the WTC Towers

In contrast to the scenes two decades earlier at the Hyatt Regency and the Kemper Arena, WTC investigators faced supreme difficulties at ground zero: a million tons of rubble, persistent fires, almost three thousand people dead, and nearby buildings so damaged that they too were threats to collapse. Nevertheless the extensive, multimillion-dollar federal investigation resulted in an authoritative report that outlined the series of events leading up to the collapse. The time and effort is well spent, contends Abolhassan Astaneh-Asl, a professor of civil and environmental engineering at the University of California, Berkeley. He says, "Understanding how and why the World Trade Center buildings collapsed will help us prevent this type of building collapse in the future."[41]

Most structural engineers considered the two WTC towers to be very sturdy buildings despite their light weight compared to similarly tall buildings. The skyscrapers' innovative, masonry-free design stacked 236 closely spaced steel columns around the building perimeter. A central core structure, with an additional 47 steel columns, housed elevators, stairwells, and utilities. The slender exterior columns gave the building flexibility while the central core bore most of the building's dead load. Steel trusses that connected the outer columns and the inner core provided stiffness while also acting as support for the concrete slab floors. This hollow-tube design meant that each acre-sized floor space was remarkably open, free of the hefty support columns found in the interior of most tall buildings.

Despite the WTC towers' extreme height (at more than 1,360 feet, they were the sixth- and seventh-tallest buildings in the world) and airy floor plans, the buildings were strong enough, with sufficient redundancy in their engineering, to resist the initial impact of being hit by speeding jets. In fact, the collapse of both buildings within two hours came as a surprise to most structural engineers. "I was shocked when they fell down, quite frankly," said New York architect David Childs, an eyewitness. "I was standing at the window when I saw this young man who works with me with this . . . this look of horror on his face, a very young man, and he said, 'Will they fall down?' I said, 'Absolutely not.'"[42]

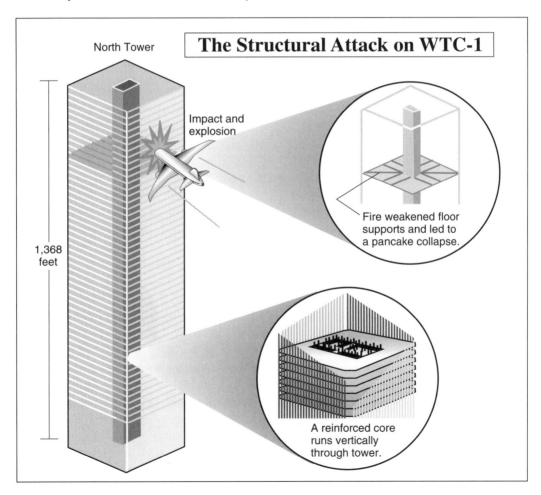

The Structural Attack on WTC-1

North Tower

Impact and explosion

Fire weakened floor supports and led to a pancake collapse.

1,368 feet

A reinforced core runs vertically through tower.

A Fatal Fire

What Childs and others in the engineering community could not know at the time was that the two buildings had suffered lethal damage resulting from the extraordinary nature of the attacks. Investigators determined that the towers might have survived the jet impacts if not for the resulting fires. When the airliners plunged into the buildings, they each took out about half of the perimeter columns on a single side (the north face of WTC-1 and the south face of WTC-2) of multiple floors. The collisions also destroyed or weakened a number of core columns in each building. Much of the airliners' highly flammable jet fuel burned off in fireballs outside of the buildings. The rest of the fuel, however, acted like starter fluid poured over furniture, equipment, and plane debris spread throughout the dozen floors worst hit.

HOW THE EMPIRE STATE BUILDING SURVIVED A PLANE CRASH

In July 1945, near the end of World War II, an American B-25 bomber flying in dense, low-lying clouds accidentally crashed into the seventy-eighth and seventy-ninth floors of Manhattan's Empire State Building, then the tallest building in the world. The plane opened a twenty-by-twenty-foot hole in the side of the fourteen-year-old skyscraper. One of the plane's two engines separated from the fuselage and tore all the way through the building and out the other side. It then hurtled over Thirty-third Street and crashed onto the roof of a twelve-story building, causing a fire. The other engine fell into an elevator shaft and collided with the top of an unoccupied elevator in the basement. Otherwise, damage was limited to the two upper floors. The three-person aircraft crew and eleven people in the building died, and two dozen more were injured, but the fire was contained and the building survived.

In reconstructing the accident, investigators were able to prove that the skyscraper was never in danger of collapse. Even traveling at 250 miles per hour, the 12-ton plane could not generate enough force to significantly budge the 365,000-ton building. The Empire State Building's many interior structural columns, and its steel-reinforced concrete floors, were able to accept the additional load from the loss of one steel supporting beam. Because the building's beams are encased in concrete, they resisted fire well. This incident, however, may have helped to create unrealistic expectations about the ability of other skyscrapers, such as the WTC towers, to survive impacts with much larger, faster, and more fuel-laden airliners.

◀ A huge section of WTC-2 plunges into a neighboring building on September 11, 2001.

The explosive impact probably destroyed sprinkler systems and knocked fireproofing off of some structural elements. The raging fire was not hot enough to melt steel supports but it did weaken them. It also weakened the angle clips that connected floor trusses to perimeter and core columns. Moreover, temperature differentials between parts of steel supports caused them to warp and bend, with perimeter columns on some floors bowing outward. Steel floor trusses no doubt sagged in the heat. In such a multiple-failure scenario, the collapse of an entire floor was almost inevitable. Once one floor fell, the weakened lower floors could not support the added weight, resulting in the ten-second progressive pancaking that left each building a smoking pile of rubble.

Engineers have pointed to a number of reasons for why WTC-2 collapsed fifty-six minutes after attack, compared to one hundred minutes for WTC-1. Flight 175 hit WTC-2 at a lower point, causing more weight to bear down on the weakened floors. Flight 175 also hit the building face somewhat off-center, compromising a corner of the inner core. Slow motion replays of the WTC-2 collapse show that the upper section of the building tipped slightly to one side before plunging like a piston into the rest of the building.

Practical Recommendations

NIST's thorough investigations of the WTC towers and the Pentagon concluded with a number of useful guidelines for reforming engineering and building practices in order to prevent building collapses and to reduce injuries and deaths when they do occur. Recommendations addressed changes to building codes set by state and local governments, engineering practices, and how buildings are designed and maintained. Investigative researchers focused not only on technical issues such as the behavior of fireproofing materials but also on "the behavior and fate of occupants and responders—both those who survived and those who did not." NIST says that this information "will be analyzed to study the movement of people during the evacuations, decision-making and situation awareness, and issues concerning persons with disabilities."[43]

According to Thomas W. Eagar and Christopher Musso, authors of an engineering journal article on the WTC collapse, "It would be impractical to design buildings to withstand the fuel load induced by a burning commercial airliner." They declare, "Instead of saving the building, engineers and officials should focus on saving the lives of those inside by designing better safety and evacuation systems."[44] The owners of the World Trade Center towers had already begun to address issues such as emergency communication systems, and how to alert building occupants about the quickest way to evacuate a building, in response to the terrorist bomb that exploded on the second level of the parking basement on February 26, 1993.

The subsequent terrorist attack on the Murrah Federal Building in Oklahoma City showed that building structure should not be overlooked as an important factor in preventing deadly collapses. In many cases, saving the building is the basis for saving the human lives.

CHAPTER FIVE

Preventing Building Collapses

A number of notable buildings have defied time and nature to remain standing for remarkable durations. The architects of ancient buildings such as the Pantheon, a monumental temple almost two millennia old and still standing proudly in Rome, and the Hagia Sophia, a fifteen-hundred-year-old church in Istanbul, Turkey, were among the earliest to recognize the inherent structural strength of the dome. Ancient engineers in Japan also had some useful insights for constructing buildings, such as the thirteen-hundred-year-old temples that are the oldest wooden buildings in the world, that could make it through an earthquake without disastrously collapsing.

Many of the world's oldest buildings have survived through some combination of craftsmanship, preservation, and historical luck. Enhancing buildings' ability to remain erect, over time and through crises like earthquakes, is also a matter of design, materials, and technology. Promising recent advances include high-tech monitoring devices that can warn of an imminent collapse. But structural engineering for long-term safety also includes inherently societal factors, from the establishment of more effective construction practices and building codes to the continued development of engineering ethics.

Designing for Longevity

Humanity has been concerned with preventing building collapses for millennia. The ancient Egyptians made a crucial design change in their pyramids after an early one, at Meidum, began to prematurely fall apart. Its outer layer now a pile of rubble, Meidum was apparently constructed with defects corrected in later pyramids: Its foundation was built on sand rather than on underlying rock, and the interior support blocks were placed level rather than inclined slightly in toward the center of the structure. "Thus two relatively minor design decisions were responsible for the catastrophe," say Matthys Levy and Mario Salvadori, "since a sandy soil magnifies the earthquake forces and setting the casings horizontally made it easier for them to slide out and fall to the ground."[45]

The devastating power of earthquakes is a major reason why some pyramids have survived to modern times but few other ancient buildings have. The Great Pyramid of Khufu, for example, is the only surviving structure among the "Seven Wonders of the Ancient World," with two of the three true buildings in the group (the other structures are a hanging garden and two colossal statues) succumbing mainly to earthquakes. The Lighthouse of Alexandria, Egypt, was seventeen hundred years old when earthquakes finally leveled it in the fourteenth century. The Mausoleum at Halicarnassus was even older when it fell to both earthquakes and dismemberment (to build a castle) circa 1500. (The other "Wonder" building, the Temple of Artemis at Ephesus, built by the

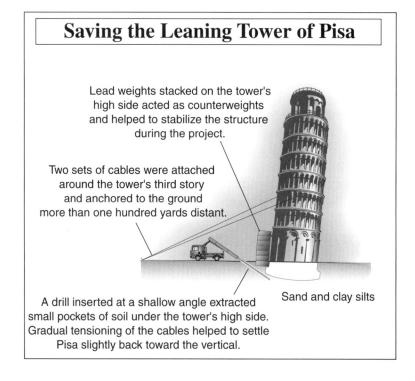

Saving the Leaning Tower of Pisa

Lead weights stacked on the tower's high side acted as counterweights and helped to stabilize the structure during the project.

Two sets of cables were attached around the tower's third story and anchored to the ground more than one hundred yards distant.

A drill inserted at a shallow angle extracted small pockets of soil under the tower's high side. Gradual tensioning of the cables helped to settle Pisa slightly back toward the vertical.

Sand and clay silts

AN IMMINENT COLLAPSE AVERTED IN ITALY

In 1990 the Leaning Tower of Pisa, one of the most dramatic buildings in the world, had to be closed to tourists. The lean on the beautiful, marble-faced structure had become so pronounced that officials feared it might crash to the ground at any time. "It was very, very close to falling over," according to British engineering professor John Burland. "It was so close that we actually couldn't get it to stand up in our computer model." A heavy wind or a minor quake could have easily been the last straw for the 180-foot-tall bell tower.

Some of the remedies that had been tried during previous centuries had worsened the situation, and Pisa's protectors moved cautiously during the 1990s. Loading hundreds of tons of lead weights onto the high side of the tower's base, and attaching long steel cables to the third story, was a temporary but unsightly fix. Scientists finally devised a more permanent and invisible solution: They slowly removed soil from under the tower's high side, allowing the building to settle slightly back toward the perpendicular by about seventeen inches. An imminent collapse averted, the Leaning Tower of Pisa was reopened to tourists with fanfare in December 2001.

Greeks in what is now western Turkey, was more than nine hundred years old when it was torn down around A.D. 400.)

These ancient, long-lived buildings shared the same basic design, with numerous sturdy stone columns supporting a heavy roof. New designs brought new challenges. Roman builders discovered the dome around A.D. 100, allowing more open interior space and dramatically taller ceilings. Over the past millennium engineers have designed increasingly elaborate towers, despite their construction often outpacing engineering—or geological—knowledge. Italy's famous Leaning Tower of Pisa, for example, began to tip over even during the tower's construction eight hundred years ago. Engineers eventually identified the reason for the structure's lean: It was built on sandy soil. By the end of the twentieth century, the entire building had sunk almost nine feet down, and its pronounced lean had reached the point where the top was some sixteen feet displaced from the base. Only an innovative engineering project managed to save it from certain collapse.

These remarkable buildings managed extraordinary life spans in spite of the limited formal knowledge about loads and stresses their builders had. Architects and engineers have learned from these and other buildings, and now have a much better understanding of what makes a building strong.

This knowledge is being incorporated into the plans for new buildings, but it is also being applied to existing buildings much less famous than Pisa, particularly to buildings in known earthquake zones.

Earthquake Engineering

In recent years earthquake engineering has increasingly embraced the guideline that it is acceptable for a building to suffer from some structural damage during an earthquake but that it should not be acceptable for a building to collapse. The $100-billion price tag for repairing damage from the Kobe earthquake, and the devastating earthquakes that struck Turkey in August 1999, India in January 2001, and Iran in December 2003, collapsing tens of thousands of buildings and killing eighty thousand people, have prompted a new sense of urgency among building designers and engineers worldwide. Earthquake-related construction standards and techniques are a major issue in the United States, where some 90 million people live in earthquake zones. According to Chris Poland, president of the federally funded Earthquake Engineering Research Institute (EERI), which studies the performance of earthquake-affected buildings and identifies practical improvements in design and construction methods:

> We know that even a moderate earthquake in a major U.S. city is going to cause economic havoc and have worldwide consequences. A decade ago, the attitude among engineers and building officials was that it was enough to keep buildings from collapsing. While this standard has saved many lives, it has failed to prevent staggering economic losses. We need to do more.[46]

Engineers in recent years have gained a greater understanding of how earthquakes affect structures and what must be done to design and construct buildings that can remain standing through an earthquake. First, a building needs to be designed with sufficient redundancy, so that the loss of a single structural element does not lead to a progressive collapse. The design should also have what engineers call continuity, meaning that a load, such as the shaking from a quake, is able to be transferred in a continuous path from one building element to another. For example, if a house's frame is poorly anchored to its foundation, the lack of continuity at that point can allow a quake to separate the two elements and wreck the house. Similarly, nonstructural elements, such as a sky-

scraper's facade, need to be firmly tied in to the building's frame. Finally, buildings simply need to be built with some level of reserve strength. Structural flimsiness was one of the main problems with the wooden houses that were readily toppled by the Kobe earthquake and with the mud-brick homes that crumbled during the 2003 Iran earthquake.

Some of the steps for preventing earthquake damage are surprisingly simple, especially for residential structures. In California, for example, because broken gas lines from water heaters that have tipped over during an earthquake are a major cause of fires, the law requires that water heaters be braced to a wall. Other steps that homeowners can take to prevent quake-related collapses include making sure that house frames are anchored to foundations, stud walls are sufficiently braced, and masonry walls or foundations are reinforced. The cost to homeowners for these projects ranges from a few hundred to tens of thousands of dollars, but such costs are dwarfed by the potential destruction of the home during an earthquake.

The Promise of Retrofitting

Earthquake retrofitting of commercial office buildings has increased in California and other areas at high risk for seismic activity. Reinforced concrete columns that are lacking sufficient rebar can be enclosed in "steel jacketing," a type of structural wrapping. New steel or reinforced concrete columns can also be added to existing masonry buildings, or such buildings can be wrapped horizontally with cables that provide strength by tying the masonry elements together. Because many buildings collapse during earthquakes due to beams detaching from columns, new methods have been developed to reinforce beam-to-column joints. Seismic upgrading can be expensive, however, and as a result it is often reserved for important public or historic buildings. Even with extensive retrofits, of course, there is no guarantee that the building will survive an earthquake undamaged. At least in most cases, a deadly progressive collapse will be avoided.

New construction for earthquake readiness may involve various techniques. The two basic approaches are to improve the performance of structural elements such as beams and columns, and to protect the entire building. An example of strengthening a structural element to better resist strong shaking is adding extra rebar inside reinforced concrete columns. Additional steel rods are now installed horizontally, wrapped around columns and hooked into the vertical bars.

▼ Construction workers add extra rebar in the basement of San Francisco's City Hall to help protect the building from quake damage.

The so-called base isolation technologies are examples of whole-building approaches to seismic protection. The idea is to separate the building foundation from the ground. In effect, the building is put on springs or shock absorbers—the earth may quake, but the building just vibrates a little.

These advances are important as they have been accompanied by recent breakthroughs in assessing building collapse risk in urban, earthquake-prone areas. Using sophisticated computer software and mapping techniques, scientists can now predict earthquake damage over a city area by analyzing soil conditions, building materials, and site characteristics. Such efforts can help earthquake professionals close what a National Academy of Sciences report after the Loma Prieta earthquake in California in October 1989 identified as "the gap between what is known and what is used, between researchers and practitioners."[47]

Buildings Go on the Defensive

The lessons that engineers have been learning about earthquake proofing have also recently begun to be used to address the growing threat of terrorist bombing. As structural engineer Ronald O. Hamburger noted after the September 11, 2001, terrorist attacks on the WTC towers and the Pentagon, "Just as structural redundancy, continuity and toughness are key to the performance of buildings in earthquakes, these same properties were key to the performance of buildings in New York and Virginia and, indeed, were key to the avoidance of even more staggering losses."[48]

The same could not be said about the 1995 Oklahoma City bombing. The fertilizer bomb constructed by Timothy McVeigh was crude but powerful—equivalent to about four thousand pounds of TNT. It exploded in a rented truck parked about fifteen feet from the front of the nine-story Murrah Federal Building. The blast carved a seven-foot-deep crater in the street and hit the mostly glass-fronted building with a powerful shock wave. Blast effects, however, killed relatively few—perhaps only 20 to 30—of the 169 victims. The bulk of the fatalities were due to the structure and design of the building. The bomb destroyed three of the building's six major structural columns, leading to a progressive collapse of approximately half of the building's floor area. It was this collapse that was fatal to many of the building's inhabitants and, ultimately,

▲ Engineers W. Gene
Corley (left) and
Jonathan Barnett outline
the lessons of Oklahoma
City and September 11,
2001, before a
congressional committee
in May 2002.

to the structure itself—what was left of it was razed five weeks later. According to forensic engineer W. Gene Corley:

> One of the key findings from our team's report was that if the 1976 Murrah building had been built using today's seismic building design details, as much as 50 to 80 percent of the structural damage, and presumably the fatalities, could have been prevented. The resulting additional construction costs [for the seismic details] would not have been millions, but a few thousand dollars.[49]

The Oklahoma City disaster underscored the need for a more assertive public policy toward preventing progressive collapses. Government officials around the world have been aware of the issue since the well-publicized partial collapse of Ronan Point in Great Britain in 1968. Until Oklahoma City, however, at least in the United States, building guideline regulations mostly paid lip service to the problem, basically admonishing designers that buildings should not suffer from a collapse that is out of proportion to the initiating damage.

Oklahoma City's legacy has thus been a renewed focus on how buildings, especially public buildings, can be better protected and built to minimize the likelihood of collapse due to bombing. A number of approaches are being pursued, both passive and active. Passive measures include setting up obstacles, such as fountains or other barriers, that create a "terrorist keep-out zone." Active measures go to the heart of good design by addressing issues such as adding redundancy and increasing the strength of beam-to-column connections. The structure of a building's facade is a more difficult issue. Fewer openings, and less glass, translates into lives saved from an explosion. But most people are unwilling to accept the trade-off of working in a dark, bunker-like environment.

Monitoring for Failure

A recent study of building collapses determined that most buildings, like the two WTC towers, cannot be expected to withstand an attack by a fully loaded jet or a military missile. Turning public buildings, in particular, into specially hardened fortresses is controversial. Another approach is the development of new monitoring and alarm systems that can warn about catastrophic failures before they happen, both during construction and after a building is completed. For example, antiterrorist researchers say that one of the potential innovations that could save lives is attaching cheap load sensors to structural members in a building. These devices could record forces and thus possibly warn of an impending

THE PENTAGON'S STURDY STRUCTURE SAVED LIVES

An engineering investigation into the September 11, 2001, jumbo jet attack on the Pentagon found that the building's framework of sturdy columns and beams helped to prevent the progressive collapse that doomed the Murrah Federal Building and the WTC towers. Traveling 530 miles per hour at impact, the airliner penetrated more than one hundred yards into the Pentagon and killed 125 occupants. Yet in the innermost sections people on the third to fifth floors were unharmed even as the plane crashed through the building beneath them.

The Pentagon benefited from an accident of history: The U.S. War Department built it in the early 1940s with the idea that it might be converted to a warehouse after the end of World War II. Workers made floors and walls especially strong to carry heavy loads. The building's first major upgrade, begun in the late 1990s, turned out to be timely—renovations in the area of the September 11 impact had just recently been completed. Structural improvements to the exterior wall, including installation of blast-resistant windows, may have limited casualties.

A LASER BEAM FOR ROOF BEAMS

After more than eight feet of snow fell on the Boston area during the winter of 1993–1994, supermarket facilities manager Steve Lee and roofing company executive Jeff Canty decided to join forces and tackle the problem of how to predict roof collapses. Lee's company was spending lots of money shoveling snow off of its flat-topped buildings, with little but intuition to rely upon to assess the level of danger from a certain load. The two men formed Safe Roof Systems of Mattapoisett, Massachusetts, to manufacture an innovative solution they hit upon: a laser-based monitoring system, dubbed the Senteck DMD-1000, that can detect a dangerous bend in a roof beam. A laser-generating device installed on the underside of a roof passes a beam of concentrated light through a series of target monitors on the midpoint of structural girders. If weight from water, snow, or ice deflects any of the girders, causing the roof to approach 70 percent or so of its carrying capacity, an alarm sounds, providing the building owner time to deal with the problem. The novel device is especially recommended for flat and low-sloped roofs.

collapse. Scientists are also working on developing sensors to detect explosives in time to warn building occupants of the potential danger.

Since 2001 a joint project of NIST and the U.S. Fire Administration has field-tested various "structural collapse prediction technologies." One live test, for example, involved setting afire a lightweight steel structure at an abandoned shopping mall in Woodbridge, Virginia. Researchers were interested in determining whether highly sensitive motion detectors could pick up vibrations that could be used to alert firefighters that the building was on the verge of collapse. A second series of tests involved the use of infrared cameras (capable of detecting gradations in heat) and carbon monoxide monitors at a brick warehouse with a wood-framed roof. Federal fire engineers hope eventually to develop a precollapse warning device that could be attached to burning buildings or incorporated into building safety systems, much like smoke detectors.

Various types of specialized sensors and monitors are already being used in the engineering community. For example, when nearby underground construction worried the owners of the Federal Reserve Bank skyscraper in downtown Boston, they contacted Construction Technology Laboratories (CTL) of Skokie, Illinois. The company's structural-diagnostics engineers deployed sensors capable of monitoring the adjacent construction vibration. The company's monitors can also alert building owners to dangerous situations due to high winds, heavy snow, thermal swings, seismic events, and foundation settlement. "Make your structure intelligent!" CTL proclaims. "There's a lot it can tell you, if you just listen."[50] Full-scale monitoring may in the near future be a crucial line of defense against partial or complete collapses.

Building for the Future

Researchers at NIST and elsewhere are also actively pursuing another approach to preventing building collapses: developing a new generation of strong but lightweight materials and high-tech building methods. Important advances are being made in materials and products that can resist fire. Computers are increasingly being used to help design new composite materials, to test metals, and to predict how durable substances will be in practice. Computers are also an essential element in the movement toward more automated construction sites. Scientists at the National Construction Automation Testbed have begun to

◀ A technician uses a computer to check out a high-tech building panel that monitors structural performance.

test TETRA, a unique robotic crane that federal officials hope may soon "enable modeling, simulation, and automation of dangerous or error-prone construction tests."[51]

Improving concrete, a modern building mainstay due to its strength, plasticity, and low cost, has been a prominent focus in recent years. Concrete may sound simple but it is actually a complex material that has spawned international symposia, research centers such as Northwestern University's Center for Advanced Cement–Based Materials in Evanston, Illinois, and an abundance of highly technical scientific studies. Researchers have discovered that getting exactly the right mixture of ingredients can produce concretes that are lighter, stronger, and more durable. Scientists have also developed new high-performance composites by adding reinforcing fibers and by experimenting with new materials such as the chemical compounds known as polymers. So-called superplasticizers now allow concretes to be made with low water content.

Until the 1960s the weight of reinforced concrete limited its use in skyscrapers higher than thirty-six stories. The first high-rise supported by a reinforced concrete frame, Cincinnati's sixteen-story Ingalls Building, was greeted with suspicion when it opened in 1902. "There was not a lot of confidence that reinforced concrete would stand up,"[52] according to University of Cincinnati civil engineer Michael Baseheart. Local lore has it that after the building was finished reporters periodically gathered to see whether it would fall over. Modern concrete now provides some of the support for the tallest buildings in the world, including the current record-holding (at 1,667 feet) Taipei 101 tower in Taipei, Taiwan.

Integrating Building Codes and Regulations

The trillion-dollar-per-year construction and building industry plays a major role in the U.S. economy, yet for the most part its regulation and oversight is inefficient and fragmented. One estimate is that more than forty thousand federal, state, and local jurisdictions regulate building design, construction, and renovation. Not surprisingly, this results in an often-conflicting array of codes, standards, and laws. The regulatory chaos has long been a factor in prominent building disasters, from the calamitous 1922 Knickerbocker Theatre collapse in Washington, D.C., to the numerous design and construction weaknesses found in schools and other public buildings destroyed or damaged by the 1999 Oklahoma City tornado. To this day some important aspects of structural engineering generally remain outside of building codes, and left to the structural engineer, such as how much wind sway is allowable at the top of a tall building.

In recent years the building and construction industry, in conjunction with federal, state, and local governments, has begun to reform aspects of design, construction, and regulation. In the mid-1990s three model code organizations in the United States formed the nonprofit International Code Council. The idea was to develop a single set of comprehensive and coordinated national construction codes, the first version of which was released in 2000 as the International Building Code. There are a number of substantial advantages in developing a single set of codes, according to the ICC:

> Code enforcement officials, architects, engineers, designers and contractors can now work with a consistent set of requirements throughout the United States. Manufacturers can put their efforts into research and development rather than designing to three different sets of standards, and can focus on being more competitive in worldwide markets . . . . A single set of codes may encourage states

▼ Lax building code enforcement in Washington, D.C., was partly to blame for the tragic Knickerbocker Theatre collapse of January 1922.

THE KNICKERBOCKER THEATRE TRAGEDY

Only about four hundred of the Knickerbocker Theatre's eighteen hundred seats held patrons on the night of January 28, 1922, for the orchestra-accompanied screening of a popular silent film comedy. The Washington, D.C., facility was mostly empty because the city had experienced a rare blizzard that had dumped more than two feet of snow on the ground. Unfortunately for those inside the four-year-old building, the snow had dangerously overloaded certain structural supports. "As the orchestra leader raised his baton to signal the start of the overture," notes Norman J. Glover in *When Technology Fails*, "a dusting of plaster fell from the ceiling onto his shoulders. A crack, several inches wide, opened in the north wall of the building next to the stage. Seconds later, the roof and the eastern two-thirds of the balcony collapsed, killing ninety-five people and injuring over a hundred others."

The tragedy was due in part to lack of oversight from the local building department and to an ill-advised change in the building code. The incident prompted a number of building code reforms, including increased building permit fees to pay for more adequate building inspections. The city also began to require that plans be submitted to a city-approved inspector before the construction of large buildings and places of public assembly.

and localities that currently write their own codes or amend the model codes to begin adopting the International Codes without technical amendments. This uniform adoption would lead to consistent code enforcement and higher quality construction.[53]

One new feature directly addresses the issue of building safety and the potentially disastrous consequences of collapses, whether from earthquake or structural failure. The new code offers a table for determining the level of risk a building faces, so that code issues (such as when an existing building should be made to comply with current code, as opposed to the code in existence when it was built) could be adaptable. For example, agricultural buildings are put in a low-risk category, since they are only occasionally occupied and would be unlikely to kill a large number of people in the event of failure. Buildings facing stricter code regulations include major facilities, such as hospitals, where significant damage could risk many lives.

Facing an Ethical Challenge

Even the best codes are effective only if the humans who must be relied upon to implement them are honest and diligent. Architects and construction engineers make life-and-death decisions when they build a structure, and the potential for disaster increases if unethical practices are rampant. Insufficient concern about ethical choices has often been a factor in building collapses, from the Knickerbocker Theatre to Sampoong. At least one prominent building, on the other hand, may have avoided disaster because of an engineer's ethics.

The noted structural engineer William LeMessurier was hailed for his innovative design when the Citicorp Tower, Citibank's planned New York City headquarters, was completed in 1977. LeMessurier's firm had served as a principal design and construction consultant for the fifty-nine-story building, which had a somewhat radical design. To leave room for a church under one corner, the tower was built on massive, nine-story support columns that descended from the middle of the skyscraper's walls, rather than at the corners. LeMessurier had combined an innovative cross-bracing scheme with a rooftop damping system—heavy blocks that moved in one direction or another to counter wind-induced sway.

Within a year of the building's acclaimed opening, however, LeMessurier found himself facing an ethical challenge. Alerted to the fact that structural supports in the building had been bolted, rather than welded, as the original design called for, he ran some new wind tests. To his alarm, they suggested that hurricane-force winds, like those that could be expected to strike midtown Manhattan once every sixteen years, might cause a structural joint in the building to pull apart. This could actually cause a total structural failure—the building might collapse.

LeMessurier knew that repairing the problem was going to be time-consuming and inconvenient for the building's owners and occupants. He also realized that his firm would be blamed for the problem, putting his professional career and reputation at stake. He nevertheless did not hesitate to take the ethical step of immediately alerting all involved to the potential problem. He convinced owners, insurance agents, and city officials that the costly repairs would be necessary. They were duly undertaken, and the building remains today one of New York's architectural highlights.

▶ Because of faulty construction, the innovative, side-column-support design of New York's Citicorp Tower created an ethical challenge for the buliding's engineer.

A Put-the-Public-First Code

If anything, LeMessurier's professional reputation was enhanced rather than harmed by his forthright willingness to act in an ethical manner. The move ultimately did not even cause his insurance company, which had to pay $2 million to Citibank, to raise LeMessurier's liability premium. A course in engineering ethics notes:

> At a meeting with officials from the insurance company, LeMessurier's secretary was able to convince them that LeMessurier had "prevented one of the worst insurance disasters of all time!" Far from behaving in an incompetent or devious manner, LeMessurier had acted in a commendable way: he had discovered an unforeseen problem, acted immediately, appropriately, and efficiently to solve it, and solved it. LeMessurier's handling of the Citicorp situation

increased his reputation as an exceptionally competent, forthright structural engineer. It also prompted his liability insurers to lower his premium.[54]

The professional responsibility and ethical behavior LeMessurier showed is increasingly crucial among structural engineers as skyscrapers soar higher and public buildings accommodate tens of thousands of people. Codes developed by professional organizations, including ASCE and the National Society of Professional Engineers, have made it clear that engineers' obligation to protect the public takes precedence over other concerns. In the ASCE's Code of Ethics, for example, the very first of five "fundamental canons" for consulting engineers maintains that "engineers shall recognize that the lives, safety, health and welfare of the general public are dependent upon engineering judgments, decisions, and practices incorporated into structures."[55]

Learning from Failure

LeMessurier faced an ethical crisis in part because he was working at the edge of existing knowledge. No building like the Citicorp Tower had been attempted before, and exactly what was required to keep it standing under certain conditions was not fully known. Ultimately, architects and builders need to be able to learn from past mistakes. Building design and construction is both art and science, an inherently imprecise human endeavor that advances in part through trial and error. As engineer Henry Petroski has noted:

> What results from the design process is a thing that has unique characteristics. It can withstand the conditions for which it was designed as long as it maintains its integrity. There is usually some leeway allowed, for engineers know that operating conditions cannot be predicted with absolute certainty. Until it fails, how far beyond design conditions a system can be pushed is never fully known. But engineers do know that nothing is perfect, including themselves. As careful and extensive as their calculations might be, engineers know that they can err—and that things can behave differently out of the laboratory.[56]

Petroski has also noted that, just as an unwillingness to take chances and to acknowledge mistakes can be a barrier to further progress, so can legal agreements that restrict public access to information about building failures. A prominent

▶ Boston's John Hancock Tower needed to be patched with plywood in 1973 when its windows began to fall off the side of the building.

example is the lid clamped onto the case of window failures at Boston's John Hancock Tower during the early 1970s. While forensic engineers have explained why the prominent building shed more than sixty of its mirrored window panels (the double-paned units, rather than the building, were at fault), the exact technical details may never be known. That is because, as part of a 1981 legal settlement, the life insurance company, glass supplier, architectural firm, general contractor, and structural engineer all pledged themselves to secrecy.

Humanity's willingness to address the age-old problem of building collapses will also require an ongoing commitment to scientific research as well as to public action. The engineering component will remain crucial as buildings face difficult new challenges, such as the trends toward replacing potentially harmful building materials with nontoxic alternatives, and toward developing more sustainable, energy-efficient building designs. Another crucial factor will be the willingness for governments, businesses, and public interest groups to continue to support engineering education and research and to fund effective building programs, codes, and regulations. Lapses in these endeavors may result in future building collapses even more tragic than those of the recent past.

Notes

Introduction: Towers of Terror

1. GECoRPA, Announcement, "2nd International Symposium on Building Pathology, Durability, and Rehabilitation: Learning from Errors and Defects in Building," November 6–8, 2003. www.gecorpa.pt.

Chapter 1: The Sound and the Fury

2. Quoted in *NOVA Online*, "Above the Impact: A Survivor's Story," Why the Towers Fell, www.pbs.org.

3. *Newsday.com*, "Excerpts of 9-11 Port Authority Calls," August 28, 2003. www.newsday.com.

4. Quoted in John Cloud, "A Miracle's Cost," *Time*, September 1, 2002. www.time.com.

5. Cloud, "A Miracle's Cost."

6. Cloud, "A Miracle's Cost."

7. Quoted in Jessica Kowal, "'The Pile' Holds Out Little Hope," *Newsday.com*, September 13, 2001. www.newsday.com.

8. Women in the Fire Service, "Report from Ground Zero: The World Trade Center Collapse," www.wfsi.org.

9. Cloud, "A Miracle's Cost."

10. Quoted in Phillip Wearne, *Collapse: When Buildings Fall Down.* New York: TV Books, 1999, p. 102.

11. Quoted in Wearne, *Collapse*, p. 138.

12. Quoted in *BBC News*, "Chicago Balcony Collapse Kills 12," June 29, 2003. http://news.bbc.co.uk.

13. Quoted in *CBS News*, "There Was No Warning," June 30, 2003. www.cbsnews.com.

14. T.R. Reid, "Kobe Wakes to a Nightmare," *National Geographic*, July 1995, p. 131.

Chapter 2: Why Buildings Collapse

15. Quoted in Steven S. Ross and the Editors of *Engineering News-Record, Construction Disasters: Design Failures, Causes, and Prevention.* New York: McGraw-Hill, 1984, p. 294.

16. Quoted in Wearne, *Collapse*, p. 152.

17. Quoted in Wearne, *Collapse*, p. 153.

18. *Federal Emergency Management Agency*, "Statement of James Lee Witt, Director, Federal Emergency Management Agency, National Press Club, March 28, 2000." www.fema.gov.

19. Quoted in Edward Martin, "Forensic Engineers Analyze Collapses," *Triangle Business Journal*, September 15, 2000, p. 31.

20. Neil Schlager, ed., *When Technology Fails: Significant Technological Disasters, Accidents, and Failures of the Twentieth Century.* Detroit: Gale Research, 1994, p. 333.

21. Matthys Levy and Mario Salvadori, *Why Buildings Fall Down: How Structures Fail.* New York: W.W. Norton, 1994, p. 209.

22. Quoted in *BBC News*, "Nine Held over Building Collapse," May 27, 2001. http://news.bbc.co.uk.

23. Quoted in CNN.com, "Guests Describe Moment of Terror," May 25, 2001. www.cnn.com.

24. Wearne, *Collapse,* p. 100.

Chapter 3: Rescue: Danger and Urgency

25. U.K. Fire Services Search & Rescue Team, "Structural Collapse: A Guide for Emergency Personnel," www.ukfssart.org.uk.

26. B.E. Aguirre et al., "The Social Organization of Search and Rescue: Evidence from the Guadalajara Gasoline Explosion," *International Journal of Mass Emergencies and Disasters*, March 1995. www.udel.edu.

27. Kathleen J. Tierney and James D. Goltz, "Emergency Response: Lessons Learned from the Kobe Earthquake," Disaster Research Center, University of Delaware, www.udel.edu.

28. Quoted in Pat Wingert, "Washington's Heroes: On the Ground at the Pentagon on Sept. 11," *MSNBC News*, www.msnbc.com.

29. Solveig Thorvald, "Engineers and Building Collapse Response: From Mexico '85 to Oklahoma '95," *EQE Review*, Fall 1995, p. 8.

30. Quoted in *ScienceDaily Magazine*, "Expendable Microphones May Help Locate Building Collapse Survivors," January 31, 2003. www.sciencedaily.com.

31. Quoted in Emma Young, "Search and Rescue Teams Face Unprecedented Challenge," *New Scientist Online News*. www.newscientist.com.

32. Aguirre et al., "The Social Organization of Search and Rescue."

33. Clark Staten, "Building Collapse Rescue," Emergency.com. www.emergency.com.

34. Quoted in Staten, "Building Collapse Rescue."

Chapter 4: Challenging Investigations

35. Levy and Salvadori, *Why Buildings Fall Down*, p. 224.

36. Gerard Shuirman and James Slosson, *Forensic Engineering: Environmental Case Histories for Civil Engineers and Geologists*. San Diego: Academic Press, 1992, p. 1.

37. Quoted in Vicky Hendley, "The Importance of Failure," *ASEE Prism*, www.asee.org.

38. Quoted in Wearne, *Collapse*, p. 10.

39. Quoted in William K. Stevens, "Before Hotel Disaster, Walkway Swayed to the Rhythm of Dancers," *New York Times*, July 19, 1981, p. A1.

40. Ross, *Construction Disasters*, p. 406.

41. Quoted in Jean Thilmany, "Modeling One Tragedy May Prevent Other," *Mechanical Engineering-CIME*, May 2002, p. 10.

42. Quoted in *Online NewsHour*, "Behind the Collapse," May 1, 2002. www.pbs.org.

43. National Institute of Standards and Technology, "NIST's Investigation of the Sept. 11 World Trade Center Disaster," Fact Sheets, www.nist.gov.

44. Thomas W. Eagar and Christopher Musso, "Why Did the World Trade Center Collapse? Science, Engineering, and Speculation," *JOM*, December 2001. www.tms.org.

Chapter 5: Preventing Building Collapses

45. Levy and Salvadori, *Why Buildings Fall Down*, p. 21.

46. Quoted in Earthquake Engineering Research Institute, "New Realities Compound 'Urban Earthquake Risk,'" www.eeri.org.

47. Commission on Engineering and Technical Systems, "Practical Lessons from the Loma Prieta Earthquake," National Academy of Sciences, 1994, p. 5.

48. Ronald O. Hamburger, "Implications of 911 Attacks for Earthquake Engineering," Earthquake Engineering Research Institute, www.eeri.org.

49. W. Gene Corley, "Testimony of Dr. W. Gene Corley, P.E., S.E. on Security in Federal Buildings on Behalf of the American Society of Civil Engineers, U.S. House of Representatives, June 4, 1998," Federation of American Scientists, www.fas.org.

50. Construction Technology Laboratories, "Why Automated Monitoring?" www.CTLGroup.com.

51. National Institute of Standards and Technology, "A Leap in Capabilities: Automating the Construction Site," www.nist.gov.

52. Quoted in Roy Wood, "Building Has Stood the Test of Time," *Cincinnati Post*, July 28, 2003. www.cincypost.com.

53. International Code Council, "Introduction to the ICC," www.iccsafe.org.

54. Onlineethics.org, "William LeMessurier: The Fifty-Nine-Story Crisis; A Lesson in Professional Behavior," Online Ethics Center for Engineering and Science at Case Western Reserve University, http://onlineethics.org.

55. *ASCE*, "Code of Ethics," www.asce.org.

56. Henry Petroski, "Failure Is Always an Option," *New York Times*, August 29, 2003. www.nytimes.com.

Glossary

building codes: Government rules that regulate construction.

cement: A finely pulverized powder, made up of silica, lime, and other compounds, used to make concrete.

compression: A squeezing force.

concrete: A strong building material made by mixing cement, aggregate such as sand and gravel, and water.

continuity: The transference of a load in a continuous path from one building element to another.

dead load: The force put onto a building's structure due to the weight of the building itself, and anything permanently attached to it.

dome: A semispherical roof first used about two millennia ago.

dynamic load: A force put onto a building that changes quickly or suddenly, such as from a gust of wind, an explosion, or a vehicle impact.

earthquake: A sudden trembling of the earth, due to the unleashing of accumulated geologic strain, that may collapse buildings and other structures.

forensic engineering: The application of the art and science of engineering in matters relating to the legal system.

live load: The force put onto a building's structure due to the sum total of its contents, such as furniture, people, and equipment; snow on the roof is also a live load.

load: The weight or force that pushes or pulls on a building.

masonry: Brickwork, block work, and stonework.

progressive collapse: A catastrophic partial or total structural failure that results when local damage causes a chain reaction with widespread effects.

rebar: Reinforcement bar; steel rods around which concrete is poured, to strengthen the concrete once it dries.

redundancy: A building's ability to support its various loads in more than one way.

reinforced concrete: Concrete with embedded steel bars for added strength.

seismic: Relating to an earthquake.

tension: The bending and stretching forces.

truss: An assemblage of beams forming a rigid framework.

unreinforced masonry: Construction such as brick, stone, or adobe that is not aided by rebar or other structural support.

void: An open space where survivors may be found in the rubble of a collapsed building.

venturi effect: A speeding up of wind due to it being squeezed between objects, such as buildings.

wind load: A load on a building caused by wind pressure and/or suction.

For Further Reading

Books

Matthys Levy and Mario Salvadori, *Why Buildings Fall Down: How Structures Fail.* New York: W.W. Norton, 1994. A lucid work for the general reader.

Steven S. Ross and the Editors of *Engineering News-Record, Construction Disasters: Design Failures, Causes, and Prevention.* New York: McGraw-Hill, 1984. This compilation of reports and articles from a prominent construction magazine offers insights into a number of major collapses.

Mario Salvadori, *Why Buildings Stand Up: The Strength of Architecture.* New York: W.W. Norton, 1990. A useful introduction to loads, materials, designs, and other important structural concepts.

Phillip Wearne, *Collapse: When Buildings Fall Down.* New York: TV Books, 1999. A lively and readable discussion of prominent structural failures.

Periodicals

T.R. Reid, "Kobe Wakes to a Nightmare," *National Geographic,* July 1995.

Solveig Thorvald, "Engineers and Building Collapse Response: From Mexico '85 to Oklahoma '95," *EQE Review,* Fall 1995.

Internet Sources

John Cloud, "A Miracle's Cost," *Time,* September 1, 2002. www.time.com.

Tom Harris, "How Building Implosions Work," HowStuff-Works, www.howstuffworks.com.

National Institute of Standards and Technology, "NIST's Investigation of the Sept. 11 World Trade Center Disaster," Fact Sheets, www.nist.gov.

NOVA Online, "Above the Impact: A Survivor's Story," Why the Towers Fell, www.pbs.org.

Web Sites

Federal Emergency Management Agency (www.fema.gov). Offers much useful information on disaster response and emergency preparedness.

National Institute of Standards and Technology (www.nist. gov). Includes fact sheets, databases, program descriptions, and links.

Works Consulted

Books

J.E. Gordon, *The Science of Structures and Materials.* New York: Scientific American Books, 1988. A handsomely illustrated introduction to how buildings, bridges, and even living organisms support themselves against natural forces.

Henry Petroski, *To Engineer Is Human: The Role of Failure in Successful Design.* New York: St. Martin's Press, 1985. Insights on the fallibility of engineering from a perceptive insider.

Karl Sabbagh, *Skyscraper: The Making of a Building.* New York: Viking Penguin, 1989. A fascinating narrative about the problems and challenges faced during the construction of Worldwide Plaza in New York City during the 1980s.

Neil Schlager, ed., *When Technology Fails: Significant Technological Disasters, Accidents, and Failures of the Twentieth Century.* Detroit: Gale Research, 1994. Detailed summaries of various catastrophes, including a number of building collapses.

Gerard Shuirman and James Slosson, *Forensic Engineering: Environmental Case Histories for Civil Engineers and Geologists.* San Diego: Academic Press, 1992. An informative and accessible professional text.

Dennis Smith, *Report from Ground Zero.* New York: Viking Penguin, 2002. A riveting account of heroic rescue actions after the September 11, 2001, World Trade Center collapses, from a former firefighter and a best-selling author.

Periodicals

Allen A. Boraiko, "Earthquake in Mexico," *National Geographic,* May 1986.

California Seismic Safety Commission, "The Homeowner's Guide to Earthquake Safety," California Department of Education, 2002.

Commission on Engineering and Technical Systems, "Practical Lessons from the Loma Prieta Earthquake," National Academy of Sciences, 1994.

Anthony Flint, "Pentagon Structure Saved Lives," *Boston Globe*, January 24, 2003.

Edward Martin, "Forensic Engineers Analyze Collapses," *Triangle Business Journal*, September 15, 2000.

David Mark McGuigan, "Urban Search and Rescue and the Role of the Engineer: Masters of Engineering Project Report," University of Canterbury, Christchurch, New Zealand, 2002.

Michael A. Riley, "Reconnaissance Report on Damage to Engineered Structures During the May 1999 Oklahoma City Tornado," Building and Fire Research Laboratory/National Institute of Standards and Technology, 2002.

William K. Stevens, "Before Hotel Disaster, Walkway Swayed to the Rhythm of Dancers," *New York Times*, July 19, 1981.

Jean Thilmany, "Modeling One Tragedy May Prevent Other," *Mechanical Engineering-CIME*, May 2002.

Kumalasari Wardhana and Fabian C. Hadipriono, "Study of Recent Building Failures in the United States," *Journal of Performance of Constructed Facilities*, August 2003.

Internet Sources

B.E. Aguirre et al., "The Social Organization of Search and Rescue: Evidence from the Guadalajara Gasoline Explosion," *International Journal of Mass Emergencies and Disasters*, March 1995. www.udel.edu.

ASCE, "Code of Ethics." www.asce.org.

BBC News, "Chicago Balcony Collapse Kills 12," June 29, 2003. http://news.bbc.co.uk.

———"Nine Held over Building Collapse," May 27, 2001. http://news.bbc.co.uk.

CBS News, "There Was No Warning," June 30, 2003. www.cbsnews.com.

CNN.com, "Guests Describe Moment of Terror," May 25, 2001. www.cnn.com.

Construction Technology Laboratories, "Why Automated Monitoring?" www.CTLGroup.com.

Doug Copp, "Survival in Earthquake—Collapsed," American Rescue Team, www.amerrescue.org.

W. Gene Corley, "Testimony of Dr. W. Gene Corley, P.E., S.E. on Security in Federal Buildings on Behalf of the American Society of Civil Engineers, U.S. House of Representatives, June 4, 1998," Federation of American Scientists, www.fas.org.

Thomas W. Eagar and Christopher Musso, "Why Did the World Trade Center Collapse? Science, Engineering, and Speculation," *JOM,* December 2001. www.tms.org.

Earthquake Engineering Research Institute, "New Realities Compound 'Urban Earthquake Risk,'" www.eeri.org.

Federal Emergency Management Agency, "Statement of James Lee Witt, Director, Federal Emergency Management Agency, National Press Club, March 28, 2000." www.fema.gov.

GECoRPA, Announcement, "2nd International Symposium on Building Pathology, Durability, and Rehabilitation: Learning from Errors and Defects in Building," November 6-8, 2003. www.gecorpa.pt.

Debra Gordon, "Expert Warns of Danger in the Dust of New York," *InteliHealth,* September 13, 2001. www.intelihealth.com.

Stephen Gottlieb, "Old or New, Facades Face Risks," *Building Operating Management,* April 2001. www.facilitiesnet.com.

Ronald O. Hamburger, "Implications of 911 Attacks for Earthquake Engineering," Earthquake Engineering Research Institute, www.eeri.org.

Vicky Hendley, "The Importance of Failure," *ASEE Prism,* www.asee.org.

International Code Council, "Introduction to the ICC," www.iccsafe.org.

Jessica Kowal, "'The Pile' Holds Out Little Hope," *Newsday.com*, September 13, 2001. www.newsday.com.

Randolph Langenbach, "Bricks, Mortar, and Earthquakes: Historic Preservation vs. Earthquake Safety," Conservationtech.com, www.conservationtech.com.

National Institute of Standards and Technology, "A Leap in Capabilities: Automating the Construction Site," www.nist.gov.

Newsday.com, "Excerpts of 9-11 Port Authority Calls," August 28, 2003. www.newsday.com.

Onlineethics.org, "William LeMessurier: The Fifty-Nine-Story Crisis; A Lesson in Professional Behavior," Online Ethics Center for Engineering and Science at Case Western Reserve University, http://onlineethics.org.

Online NewsHour, "Behind the Collapse," May 1, 2002. www.pbs.org.

Henry Petroski, "Failure Is Always an Option," *New York Times*, August 29, 2003. www.nytimes.com.

ScienceDaily Magazine, "Expendable Microphones May Help Locate Building Collapse Survivors," January 31, 2003. www.sciencedaily.com.

Clark Staten, "Building Collapse Rescue," Emergency.com. www.emergency.com.

Kathleen J. Tierney and James D. Goltz, "Emergency Response: Lessons Learned from the Kobe Earthquake," Disaster Research Center, University of Delaware, www.udel.edu.

U.K. Fire Services Search & Rescue Team, "Structural Collapse: A Guide for Emergency Personnel," www.ukfssart.org.uk.

Pat Wingert, "Washington's Heroes: On the Ground at the Pentagon on Sept. 11," *MSNBC News*, www.msnbc.com.

Robert Winston, "Boston Firefighters Narrowly Escape Death," Fire Reports, Boston Fire Department, www.ci.boston.ma.us.

Women in the Fire Service, "Report from Ground Zero: The World Trade Center Collapse," www.wfsi.org.

Roy Wood, "Building Has Stood the Test of Time," *Cincinnati Post*, July 28, 2003. www.cincypost.com.

Emma Young, "Search and Rescue Teams Face Unprecedented Challenge," *New Scientist Online News*, www.newscientist.com.

Web Sites

American Society of Civil Engineers (www.asce.org). Among the useful features from the site for this leading trade association are research resources, news and alerts, and professional issues.

Earthquake Engineering Research Institute (www.eeri.org). Offers abstracts of journal articles, earthquake basic briefs, CDs, publications, and more.

iCivilEngineer (www.icivilengineer.com). "The Internet for Civil Engineers" site provides an up-to-date engineering failure watch that summarizes building collapses around the world.

National Information Service for Earthquake Engineering (http://nisee.berkeley.edu). Offers images of historical earthquakes, an abstracts database, engineering reports, and more.

National Institute of Building Sciences (www.nibs.org). Includes a hazards loss–estimation program, a "whole building design guide," and papers from a workshop on prevention of progressive collapse.

Index

Picture Credits

About the Author

Mark Mayell is a freelance writer and editor who has authored nonfiction books on health and travel, as well as titles in the Man-Made Disasters series on nuclear accidents and tragedies of space exploration. He lives with his wife and two children in Wellesley, Massachusetts.

DATE DUE